ATTENTION
MAILROOM
FROM: THE PUBLISHER

KITTY KAT DOES NOT CONTAIN:
Shout Outs from Inmates
Inmate Addresses
No Nudity or Sexual Acts
Descriptions of Violent Acts
Articles About Making Weapons or Hooch
Articles About Drugs, Escapes, or Smuggling Contraband

Freebird Publishers
www.FreebirdPublishers.com

Freebird Publishers
221 Pearl St., Ste. 541
North Dighton, MA 02764

Please feel free to contact us with your concerns.
Diane@FreebirdPublishers.com

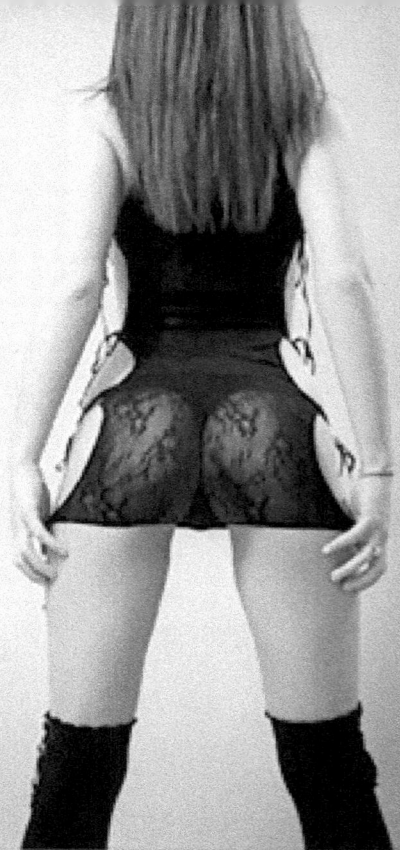

Kitty Kat

ADULT ENTERTAINMENT NON-NUDE RESOURCE BOOK

REVISED EDITION

BY MIKE ENEMIGO

Producer of The Cell Block
Revised by Freebird Publishers

Freebird Publishers
www.FreebirdPublishers.com

All Freebird Publishers titles, imprints and distributed lines are available at special quantity discounts for bulk purchases for sales promotions, premiums, fund-raising, educational or institutional use

Copyright © 2017 Kitty Kat by Mike Enemigo Revised 2021
Publisher & Distributor: Freebird Publishers
221 Pearl St., Ste. 541 North Dighton, MA 02764
Web: FreebirdPublishers.com
E-Mail: diane@freebirdpublishers.com
Text: 774-406-8682
Send Letters to the Editor to the above address

ISBN-10: 0-9913591-6-X
ISBN: 978-0-9913591-6-5

Editor / Publisher	Freebird Publishers
Producer	The Cell Block
Cover Designs	Cyber Hut Designs
Advertising	diane@freebirdpublishers.com
Wholesale	diane@freebirdpublishers.com
Authorized Distributors	FreebirdPublishers.com
	TheCellBlock.net
	Amazon.com

DISCLAIMER

This publication is designed to provide accurate and authoritative information with regard to the subject matter covered. NOTE: This book is a reference guide; information contained herein is based on information provided by the businesses. The Publisher and Editors make no warranties or claims that any business is obligated to provide any service(s) to any person(s).

FIND THE SEXY PRODUCT SELLERS YOU NEED **FAST**.

Kitty Kat

TABLE OF CONTENTS

Mike Enemigo Producer of The Cell Block

To All Our Readers

We have edited our directory to include the most up-to-date information on all the listings. We research and contact each and every business that is listed in our directory. We have updated, edited and corrected all the reputable businesses in our business directory of resources. As we all know this is a never-ending project. We will continue to maintain our publication to be comprehensive and accurate for better quality that you can count on. We at Freebird Publishers greatly appreciate the assistance of our readers. Your efforts truly matter to help us maintain accurate updates in our publications. In order for us to confirm that a company is a Return to Sender (RTS) we need to see the original front or a copy of the RTS envelope. When you send in a review of a company, please remember to be direct, short and to the point. When sending in new companies you have currently ordered from send us all the information you have on them and a couple of sentences on what they offer. If you have any extra materials, please include. Thank you for your interest in our publications and support. As always, be strong, stay safe and know you are not forgotten.

Respectfully,

Freebird Publishers

Best Business Practices

A good rule of thumb when dealing with any mail order business that you or friends have not recently done business with, is to send a SASE with simple request for information. This will tell you a few things. First, how long did it take to get a response, which gives you a good idea on how long an order will take. Secondly, the quality and ease of reading/understanding the information you received, which tells you the level of the business's professionalism. Finally, if you never get a response, you have cut your losses and only wasted the price of a couple of stamps.

Sexy Photos
Non-Nude

4 The Pack Entertainment

PO Box 4057
Windsor Locks, CT 06096

Provide a vast array of services most of which will be aimed at making those who are incarcerated days a little better. Offer package of flyers for $3. Non-nude photos $0.50 each, no minimum, shipped in envelopes of no more than 25 per, shipping is $1 per envelope. In addition, they have Private Stock Photos, Internet Models and Celebrity Photos and Professional Photo Shoots.

Web: 4thepackentertainment.com
Email: 4thepackentertainment@gmail.com

7 Star Photos

602 N. Main St. #7
Lansing, KS 66043

They have three different flyers that each come with two photos for $5 each. Categories: PG, RR and XXX. Photos are $1 each. Each order must have $2 shipping included. They require an outside address so the prison can return any rejected photos to that address and not the company. Payment by checks and money orders only and ever order or letter must include a SASE.

Phone: 816-343-4201
Email: 7starphotos@gmail.com

Acme Publications

PO Box 130300
St. Paul, MN 55113

"They have pictures of beautiful celebrities. They are sold in 4x6 size on high quality photo paper for $0.35 cents each. 8x10 are $1.00 each, 5x7 are $0.65 cents each. (For example, if there are 2 pictures for a person, each picture is $0.35 cents. You don't have to buy the whole set.) Try some. If you would like to have pictures of your favorite celebrities, don't put it off, start your collection now, ORDER TODAY. Money back guarantee.

Order 22 photos and get 4 free. Order 35 photos and get 12 free. Order 100 photos and get 50 free. Order 200 photos and get 150 free. And always free shipping.

Review: The catalog I have has a lot of older celebrity pictures; Marilyn Monroe, Demi Moore, Kate Moss, old-school pictures of R&B star Mya, etc. It has other stuff, too, though. See the full list of 306 girls later in the book. - Mike

Branlettes Beauties

PO Box 5765
Baltimore, MD 21282

Their prices are simple:

- ✪ 1-4999 photos: $0.45 cents each 5000 plus photos equals 20 discount
- ✪ 1-9 catalogs: $3.00 each (plus SASE)
- ✪ 10 catalogs: $25.00 plus SASE (4 stamps)

Select your favorite:

White catalogs (60 volumes), Black catalogs (60 volumes), Asian and Latino catalogs (60 volumes). Please state what style photos - provocative poses or nude.

FREE catalog? Yes. Just send us 2 First Class Forever stamps and a SASE and they will send to you one nude or BOP-friendly sample catalog (1 per customer) with 84 gorgeous girls in full color. Act now as this offer will not be around long.

Branlettes Breathless Beauties Bag: A random selection of 50 of the rare and exotic. Yes, 50 beauties all posing just for you. Plus 2 of our finest color catalogs. Only $19.99. Did you read that right? Yes, only $19.99 for 50 of Branlettes Breathless Beauties (please specify nude or BOP-friendly). Plus, two of our finest color catalogs FREE. (You pick the volumes) Their regular shipping/handling policies apply.

All sales are final. Each catalog has 84 gorgeous ladies to choose from. High quality prints on 4x6 glossy photo paper.

Shipping and handling:

Due to various prison policies regarding how many pictures can be sent in one envelope, our policy is as follows:

- ✪ 01-5 photos: $1.00 per envelope
- ✪ 06-15 photos: $1.50 per envelope
- ✪ 16-25 photos: $2.00 per envelope

Their simple policies: Special requests are not permitted and all models are of legal age. Due to tremendous time and cost answering letters, unless you are placing an order or a question regarding your order, they will not reply to any other questions. A SASE is required for any inquiries or concerns.

You and you alone are responsible for your selections being allowed into your facility. Know your institution's policies as to what image content is allowed. Returned orders are non-refundable. They will be held for 14 calendar days in order for you to send self-addressed stamped envelopes (3 First Class stamps per envelope), with a street address for every 20 pictures. All returned images held after 2 weeks will be resold and they will return them to our stock.

All payments are by institutional checks or US postal service or Western Union money orders. These payments are processed immediately and shipped in less than 3-4 weeks. Any other company money orders delay shipment 8-10 weeks or until that money clears our bank. Yes, they deal with people that are, while in prison, still trying nickel-and-dime scams.

Butterwater, LLC
PO Box 669
Mathews, NC 28106

Catalogs:

- ✪ The Butterwaters 1 & 2: $2.50 or 5 stamps (with SASE). FREE online.
- ✪ The Butterwaters 3 & 4: $2.50 or 5 stamps (with SASE). FREE online.
- ✪ The Butterwaters 5: $2.50 or 5 stamps (with SASE). FREE online.
- ✪ The Butterwaters 6: $2.50 or 5 stamps (with SASE).
- ✪ The Butterwaters 7: $2.50 or 5 stamps (with SASE).
- ✪ White Pages 1: $2.50 or 5 stamps (with SASE).
- ✪ White Pages 2: $2.50 or 5 stamps (with SASE).
- ✪ Pink #1 (nude): $5.00 or 10 stamps.
- ✪ Pink #2 (nude): $5.00 or 10 stamps.
- ✪ The "B" side: FREE online.

Send SASE today for a FREE catalog.

4x6 color photos. One dollar ($1.00) per photo. Minimum order is ten (10) photos for ten dollars ($10.00), plus $2.50 shipping and handling. Orders can be shipped as per facility rules (5 per envelope, etc.). They do not accept cash. Please send money order or facility check. Mail SASE for order form or create your own list by clearly writing on paper.

Website: thebutterwaters.com

Cellmate & Convict Services
PO Box 653
Venus, TX 76084
Web: cellmates2015.com
cellmates2015@yahoo.com

Prices are direct:

- ✪ 4x6 photos $0.50 cents each
- ✪ 5x7 photos $1.00 each
- ✪ 8x10 photos $2.00 each

Catalogs:

- ✪ 2015 Catalogs Available (send SASE for list)
- ✪ 2016 Catalogs Available (send SASE for list)
- ✪ 2017 Catalogs Available (send SASE for list)

Shipping and handling:

Due to various prison policies regarding how many pictures can be sent in one envelope, our policy is as follows:

- ✪ 01-7 photos: $0.75 per envelope
- ✪ 08-14 photos: $1.00 per envelope
- ✪ 15-21 photos: $1.50 per envelope
- ✪ 22-28 photos: $2.00 per envelope
- ✪ 29-35 photos: $2.50 per envelope
- ✪ 36-43 photos: $3.00 per envelope
- ✪ 44-51 photos: $3.50 per envelope
- ✪ 52-64 photos: $4.25 per envelope
- ✪ 65-72 photos: $5.00 per envelope
- ✪ 73-99 photos: $6.00 per envelope
- ✪ 100 plus Free if all ship in ONE pack
- ✪ or Mail SASE to cover every 6 photos

Web: cellmates2015.com
cellmates2015@yahoo.com

Chronos Masterpieces
509 Laurel #1111
La Marque, TX 77568

Offering photos in a simple way. Sets of grab bags in 27 varieties. 100 photos per set for one price of $35 plus $5 s/h for first envelope, $ per additional envelopes. Sets including Asian, Hispanic, White, Black, Small Boob, Amateur, Red-head, Blonde, Young, Selfies, Butts, Panties, Pigtails, Risque' and Mixes Women. Also have Miscellaneous Women and Men sets too! Grab bag sets only, no choosing the photos.

Email: chronosmasterpieces@outlook.com

Sexy Photos Non Nude

CNA Entertainment, LLC

PO Box 185
Hitchcock, TX 77563

They are a visual media entertainment mail order LLC that distributes photos of a large variety of models to the prison population across the country. They currently have over 200 non-nude catalogs with a variety of different themes. Topless/nude catalogs are available upon special request for states that allow them. If your state does not allow this, do not order them because you will not get them! Due to many requests for multiple catalogs, they are now offering multiple catalogs for $0.50 cents each plus $1.00 for shipping. For example, if you want 20 catalogs, it will be $5.00 plus $1.00 for a total of $6.00 Easy enough? Send a list with the ones you want from our current list and send the appropriate payment. They do not replace lost, denied, unwanted or stolen catalogs. Do not replace lost, denied, unwanted or stolen catalogs.

Their non-nude catalogs are currently:

Here are our newest sets in our newest series. The Series is called "E Series Blossoming Young Ladies" and it has 8 new models that chances are you have never seen before and this is a highly sought after series. They are more what you would call barely legal (18 and legal none the less). They will add more to this series as well as other niches soon.

- ✪ EBYA - E Series Blossoming Young Ladies - Aleksandra 1, 2 & 3 * *
- ✪ EBYC - E Series Blossoming Young Ladies - Christy 1 & 2 * *
- ✪ EBYK - E Series Blossoming Young Ladies - Katya 1 *
- ✪ EBYL - E Series Blossoming Young Ladies - Larisa 1 & 2 * *
- ✪ EBYM - E Series Blossoming Young Ladies - Mariska 1 *
- ✪ EBYS - E Series Blossoming Young Ladies - Sasha 1 & 2 * *
- ✪ EBYT - E Series Blossoming Young Ladies - Tatyana 1 & 2 * *
- ✪ EBYV - E Series Blossoming Young Ladies - Victoria 1 *
- ✪ AA-Amazing Amateurs 1 Revised & 2 * (amateur photos)
- ✪ AG-Asian Angels 1 & 2 * Revised (All Asian)
- ✪ ANE-Anime 1, 2 & 3 * (Assorted Anime Girls)
- ✪ ARM-Ample Rollie-Pollie Mommas (BBW - BIG women!!!)
- ✪ BOB-Baby Oil Bonanza Revised (All lubed up)
- ✪ BT-Bath Time 1 & 2 * Revised (Tub or shower pictures)
- ✪ BMV-Blond Model Variety 1 (Several Different Blond Models)
- ✪ BB-Black Beauties1, 2, 3 & 4 * Revised (All Black)
- ✪ BBVM-Black Beauties Model Variety 1 & 2 * (All Black model set asst)
- ✪ BCM-Black Chunky Monkeys 1 Revised (All Black thicker chicks)
- ✪ BVV-Black Voluptuous Vixens 1 Revised (Big boobed)
- ✪ T-It's All In The Toes 1 Revised, 2 & 3 * ("Cameltoe" shots)
- ✪ CL-Cheerleaders 1 Revised & 2 * (Cheerleading outfits)
- ✪ CM-Chunky Monkeys 1, 2, 3 & 4 * Revised (Thicker chicks)
- ✪ COS-Girls of Cosplay 1 & 2 * (Fantasy & gamer costumes)
- ✪ DU-Costumes 1 & 2 * Revised (Girls in costumes)
- ✪ FP-Famous People 1, 2, 3, 4, 5, 6, 7 & 8 * (Assorted Celebrities)
- ✪ FPIA - Celebrity Sets - Iggy Azalea
- ✪ FPMC-Celebrity Sets - Miley Cyrus

By Mike Enemigo

- FPSG-Celebrity Sets - Selena Gomez
- FPBP-Celebrity Sets - Betty Paige (Yeah, vintage pinup)
- FPTS-Celebrity Sets - Taylor Swift 1 & 2 *
- FPS-Famous People in Sports 1 (Celebrities in sports)
- FC-Flat to Little Bosoms 1 & 2 * (Small to no boobed females)
- FU-Fire Me Up (Females posing & smoking)
- G-Goth & Punk 1 & 2 * Revised (Goth & Punk outfits)
- GBB-Girls Behaving Badly Revised (Girls being bad girls)
- GFF-Girlfriends Forever 1 & 2 * (2 hot girls per scene)
- FF-Fresh Faces Revised (Younger females - 18 plus years old)
- GS-G-Strings 1 & 2 * Revised (Females in G-strings)
- HM-Hot Mommas 1 Revised & 2 * (MILF's/older ladies)
- HP-Hot Panties 1 & 2 * Revised (Hot & cute lil panties)
- HG-Hotties N Glasses 1 (Females wearing glasses)
- JB-Just Butts 1 Revised (Butt shots)
- JF-Just Feet 1 & 2 * (Ladies showing her feet)
- JFB-Just Feet Model Set - Beth (Beth showing her feet)
- JFE-Just Feet Model Set - Emily (Emily showing her feet)
- LL-Latina Lovers 1, 2 & 3 * Revised (Hispanic females)
- M-Male 1 Revised, 2, 3, 4-(Black), 5, 6-(Twinkish), 7-(Asian), 8, 9, 10-(Twinkish) & 11-(Twinkish), * (Male catalogs)
- MFP-Famous Guys 1, 2 & 3 (Black) (Assorted MALE Celebrities)
- MYB-Young Men Model Set - Benji - MALES (18 years old Male)
- MYH-Young Men Model Set - Hunter- MALES (18 years old Male)
- MYM-Young Men Model Set - Mikey- MALES (18 years old Male)
- MYMC-Young Men Model Set - Marcus & Carlos - MALES (19 years old Males)
- MG-Midgets - Lil' Ladies Revised (Fetish Catalog - Midgets)
- MF-Midgets & Feet Revised (Fetish Catalog - Feet & Midgets)
- NRD-Nerdy Girls (Nerd females with glasses & more)
- PRG-Pregnant Chicks (Pregnant females)
- RCC-Rednecks, Country & Cowgirls 1 & 2 * (Hot country girls)
- RH-Redheads Revised (Redheaded females)
- CG-Schoolgirls 1 & 2 * Revised (Females schoolgirl outfits)
- SLF- 1, 2, 3, 4 & 5 * Selfies (Self shots of various hotties)
- SS-Sporty Sensations (Sport scenes)
- TG-Texas Teasers (Texas style females)
- OS-The Other Side (Pregnant, Feet, Latex, Leather & Muscles)
- TBB-Thick Black Booties 1 Revised & 2 * (Black butt shots)
- TF-Thigh Highs & Fishnets (This replaces Pantyhose catalog)
- VV-Voluptuous Vixens 1 & 2 * Revised (Big boobed)
- W-Workout Wonders Revised (Working out & posing)
- WD-Wrestling Divas (Wrestling females)
- WM-Women with Muscles (Muscle bound females)
- WXS-Women of Xtreme Sports (Hot women of extreme sports)
- VS - Variety of Sexy Safe Flix 1, 2, 3,4 ,5 ,6 7, 8, 9, 10 & 11 * (Catalogs full of photos that SHOULD be completely safe in 99% of all units. Sexy shots with no bare butts (G-strings and bikinis at minimum), no cupped breast, no see-through, no girl girl, no inappropriate touching, no guys, no simulated sex or masturbation & more!)

Each Pornstar set is different so order individual catalogs by the models' name - Below are many separate catalogs

- PSA-Alexis Texas Revised -   PSAB-Audrey Bitoni - PSAG-Aria Giovanni Revised - PSAL-Aaliyha Love - PSFR-Faye Reagan 1 & 2 * - PSGS-Gia Steel 1, 2 & 3 * -   PSJF-Jada Fire - PSL-Luscious Lopez - PSLA-Latina Assortment 1 (Several Different Models) - PSML-Marie Luv - PSP-Pinky 1, 2 & 3 * -   PSSC-Sydnee Capri

Each model set is different so order individual catalogs by the models' name - Below are

Sexy Photos Non Nude

many separate catalogs

- Asian Model Sets - AMHT-Hannah & Tai Ling (2 models) - AML-Lin (22 years old) - AMNM-Nyomi & Mika (2 models) - AMS-Sunee (20 years old)
- Blonde Model Sets - BMA-Angel & Jenna Revised (19 years old) - BMS-Suzie Q & Jenna Revised (19 years old)
- Chunky Model Sets - CMC-Malibu Candy (19 years old)
- Flat Chested Model Sets - FCML-Lydia (19 years old) - FCME-Erin Nicole (20 years old)
- Fresh Faces Model Sets - FFMC-Chloe Knox 1, 2 & 3 * (18 years old)
- Latina Model Sets - LMSR-Sativa Rose
- Model Sets - FMB-Berlin (21 years old blonde) - FMD-Destiny (19 years old brunette) - FME-Eesha Revised (19 years old Indian) - FMG-Geri (20 years old black headed) FMH-Hilary (19 years old redheaded) - FMK-Katrina (20 years old blond) - FS-Katie Jordan 1 & 2 * (18 years old brunette) - FMN-Nadya - (18 years old blond) - FMV-Veronica (20 years old blond) - FMY-Yasmine (20 years old Indian)
- Hot Momma Model Sets - HMC-Courtney (MILF)
- Nubian Model Sets - NMK-Kitten (33 years old) - NML-LaShelle (19 years old) - NMV-Vanessa (19 years old)
- Redheaded Model Sets - RMC-Charisma (19 years old) - RMD-Dana (19 years old) - RML-Laura (24 years old)
- Tattooed Model Sets - TATC- Cami (18 years old) - TATM- Mason & Betty (2 solo models with large breast)
- Top Heavy Model Sets - THML-Louisa (19 years old)
- Tranny Model Sets - ETBJ-Bailey Jay * - ETMJ- Joanna Jet * - ETNN-Nody Nadia *

Below are the E Series catalogs. Make sure you add the "E" to the title when you order the catalog

- EB-Butts N Backs * Revised (Butt pictures)
- ECT-Cameltoes * 1 Revised & 2 * * (Cameltoe pictures)
- EFM-Fetish Mix 1 * (Bondage & adult diaper)
- EHP-Hot Panties 1 * Revised (Hot & cute lil panties)
- ELJ-Latina Model Sets - Jackie * (Ultra hot Latina)
- EMP-Males in Pantyhose * (Guys posing in pantyhose)
- EMK-Male Model Sets - Ken * (25 years old male pictures)
- EMS-Male Model Sets - Stefan * (22 years old male pictures)
- EMT-Male Model Sets - Tommy * (25 years old male pictures)
- EM-Men 1, 2 & 3 * * Revised (Assorted guys)
- EOF-The 'O' Face 1 Revised & 2 * * (Girls with THE look & looking back)
- EPSC-Pornstars - Cherokee Dass *
- EPSSB-Pornstars - Skyy Black *
- ERH-Redheads 1 Revised & 2 * * (Hot redheads)
- ES-Super Shots * Revised (Borderline butts & more)
- ET-Tranny 1, 2, 3, 4 & 5* * (transgenders)
- ETBH-Tranny with Bad Habits * (Four transgenders w/habits)

By Mike Enemigo

Photo prices:

Extra Large (4x6): $0.70 cents each
Special: Order 100 or more XL photos for only $0.60 cents each

Shipping:

Shipping and handling is $2.00. You may now insure your package for $3.00 EXTRA for the first envelope to make sure it gets to your prison or get it replaced. This is USPS insurance not theirs so it is a Federal crime that will be investigated if someone intercepts it or makes a false claim (mail fraud). Another choice is to put $2.00 confirmation on it to only prove that it has arrived. This is not insurance, just proof that it has arrived at your mailroom.

Additional shipping note:

States that have limits on photos per envelope will have to pay a higher shipping fee for additional envelopes used to mail your stuff. So, figure this up before you do the shipping. Let's say your prison only allows 3 pictures per envelope and you order 15 pictures. That will require 5 separate envelopes with 5 separate postages and 5 separate labels and so forth.... it is only $0.50 cents per extra envelope (that's the cost of the stamp and envelope) times the number of envelopes you need. You already know if your prison is like this so please figure your shipping accordingly. ONLY order different envelopes if you need them mailed in different envelopes. Please give instructions on how to divide your order if you do order them. Also, ALL envelopes are mailed out on the same day, but may not arrive on the same day. So, if you see, like, "1 of 15," then 15 envelopes have been mailed out. You may make your own order form or request one.

For more information about any of their services or products, please drop them a line and they will fill you in. They hope to hear from you soon and have a great day."

Website: CNAEntertainment.com
Email: CNATexas@live.com

Comment: This company has a lot going on - pictures, custom calendars, bookmarks, 20-photo "proof" sets, and more, all with bad babes on them. This is one of the biggest, most serious non-nude photo companies I've seen and they are well organized.– Mike

CurbFeelers
Box 421175
Houston, TX 77242-1175

They sell mail order photos in various categories. They carry quality photos. They are old fashion, orders by mail and accept payment by money orders, inmate checks and stamps. They have no email, website, phones, take no credit cards, Paypal etc. Write them for info include an SASE.

David Carter
Box 378
Bardwell, TX 75101

In business for five years. They sell non-nude provocative photos and service all states in the US. Offering 15 photo catalogs, bookmarks, have monthly photo subscription services and pattern catalogs. Black and white photo and pattern catalogs are $1 each or 3 forever stamps. Color photo catalogs are $3 each or 7 Forever stamps. Patterns $0.35 each, photos, $0.40 each. Accept only money orders, prison facility checks and new stamps, no singles. 3 Forever stamps are equal to $1. All checks have to be payable to David Carter only. All orders over 100 items ships

for free, otherwise S/H is $1.50 per order or per envelope needed to send ordered. Photos are 4x6 printed on gloss photo stock and high quality. Minimum order $10.

Doll Services
Box 7891
Gurnee, IL 60031

They offer a variety of adult entertainment photos, photo services starting at a $1-$3. Many bundles, samplers, packs and videos. Can or- der to be shipped by mail or by mail through Amazon. Payments accept- ed are facility checks, money orders payable to Doll only and stamps, no singles or taped accepted. (stamps not accepted on specials). They offer seasonal specials. The website is just for information, cannot take any orders. They do not offer email on the website but links the user to Messenger. The flyer is one letter size page printed on both sides with lists. Minimum order $5 all shipping included in prices.

Email: dymemagpr@yahoo.com
Web: welcometodoll.com

FIYA GIRLS
PO Box 192
Dequincy, LA 70633
Email: fiyagirls@yahoo.com

"Check us out. They are the best in the game.. Here they have the sexiest and hottest babes. They have plenty of nail-biting catalogs, with different types of breath-taking women of all races to choose from. FIYA girls catalog has the biggest selections to choose from. All photos $0.50

1. Send $6.00 or 25 stamps to receive hi gloss color catalog #19. It has over 450 white girls, coeds and Spanish girls. All hot poses in bras, G-strings and panties. It also comes with 1 FREE picture.

2. Send $6.00 or 25 stamps to receive hi gloss color catalog #18. It comes with 1 FREE picture. It has over 440 new black, white and Spanish girls. All have super big apple bottoms. You don't want to miss out on catalog 18 and 19. ALWAYS SEND AN ALTERNATE ADDRESS WITH YOUR ORDER IN CASE YOUR ORDER IS REJECTED. WE WILL SEND IT TO THE STREET ADDRESS THAT YOU PROVIDED US WITH.

3. If your jail or prison is strict on sexy photos, send $3.00 along with SASE for the get-in cat #1. They will let it in and the photos too.

4. Send $13.00 to get non-nude 10 pictures get-in set. Make sure to say if you want black or white girls when you want a get-in 10 picture set.

5. Send $20.00 to get the 30 pictures get-in set and a FREE get-in #1 cat. It contains all races wearing bikinis on beaches and beside pools. Get the all NEW supervised high gloss color VIP catalog #4. Over thousands to choose from. All races, strippers, porn stars and all... Only $15.00 (FREE S/H) includes 2 FREE pictures. Price on all pictures in VIP cat #4 is now only $1.00 each. Must choose at least 15 pictures. And send a SASE for each envelope. They ship up to 22 pictures per envelope. You need to put 2 postage stamps on each envelope.

6. ALL NUDE BIG BUNDLE CATALOG PACKAGE ONLY $15.00. Comes with FREE pictures.

7. Get mail get paid book is still only $10.00.

8. They have over 100 10 picture sets of black, white and Asian women in sets of 10 different poses. They are very hot 10 picture sets. Only $13.00 a set or you can choose 3 sets for $23.00.

9. VIP yearly membership is only $45.00.

10. Send $6.00 to get one of the hottest all white girls coed catalogs on the market -cat #11. It has over 450 to

By Mike Enemigo

choose from.

11. Cat #20 has over 400 sexy white girls to choose from. Send $6.00 to get it.

12. The 5 pack has a large selection of ebony women with apple bottoms mixed in with Asian and white women. It's hot.. Send only $7.00. It comes with 2 FREE pictures. It has hundreds to choose from.

13. 50 PICTURES OF HOT NON-NUDE WITH THE BEST QUALITY ASIANS WEARING LINGERIE AND BIKINIS FOR ONLY $25.00 FREE SHIPPING.

14. Vol. #1, 50 PICTURES OF HOT NON-NUDE BEST QUALITY MIXED SET OF WHITE, BLACK AND SPANISH GIRLS AND PORN STARS WEARING STRIPPER OUTFITS ONLY $25.00. FREE SHIPPING.

15. Vol. #2, 3, 4 AND 5 HAVE 50) Pictures SETS OF WHITE, BLACK, AND LATIN GIRLS EACH 50 PICTURE SET IS ONLY $25.00. FREE SHIPPING.

16. BUY ALL 5 GRAB BAG SETS. EACH SET HAS A MIX OF RACES. THEY ARE ONLY $25.00 A SET. FREE SHIPPING. THERE ARE A TOTAL OF 10 SETS. Vol. #1-10. BUY ALL 10 NUDE SETS AND GET 50 FREE SHOTS.

VIP cat 5 has over a couple thousand choices. Only $15.00. FREE S/H. Cats 27-32. VIP cat 6 has over a couple thousand choices only $15.00. FREE S/H

Cats 33-38). VIP cat 5 and 6 consist of white cameltoe shots, bikini shots, curvy models, petite models, Latino models, beach shots, bedroom shots, G-strings shots, miniskirts, latex, spandex, fitness models, amateur porn stars, micro thongs, booty shorts, tight jeans, blondes, redheads, brunettes, big breast, slim waist, big booties, erotic poses, college coeds, huge cameltoe. New anmie sluts. They are super-hot. VIP cat #5 and #6 are non-nude catalogs."

Review: I wrote their ad the way they wrote it so you can judge for yourself. In addition, though have seen guys get their orders from them, I ordered some pictures and the "Get Mail Get Paid" book and never got it. – Mike

Flix 4 You
PO Box 290249
Sandhills, SC 29229

"Get them cuz they're hot. Flix 4 You is often imitated, but can't be duplicated.. They offer the best quality photos and fastest service in the game. Only .75 per photo. New Deal: order 10-14 photos, get 1 photo FREE; 15-19 photos; Get 3 photos FREE; order 20-24 photos, get 5 photos FREE; order 25 or more, get 10 photos FREE. Over 100 catalogs to choose from, all just $5.00 each or 20 stamps. Black, Latin, Asian, White, celebrity, porn stars, club scenes, bikini shots, iPhone cuties, selfies and more. From fully clothed to fully nude. They offer photos that will satisfy everyone's needs..

Overstock special: 20 photos for $7.50. You choose race, front shot or back shot, and they will choose from our overstock collection. You cannot choose from any specific catalog.

Shipping and handling is $2.20 per envelope. Each envelope only holds 25 photos. If you need more

than 1 envelope, you must send additional shipping and handling. New policy as of January 1, 2015: they will no longer be responsible for rejected catalogs or photos. Be sure to order according to your facility's mailroom policy."

Review: Flix 4 You sent me a couple of their catalogs - 'insta-grammy 2' and 'Legs, Tights, Assets 2'. The catalogs are printed in color and offer several choices each. Their images are some of the best I've seen. The baddest babes on the planet. - Mike

F.O.S.
Box 42922
Phoenix, AZ 85080

In business since 8 years with excellent customer service. 50 photos at $0.50 cents each. 50 photos at $0.50 cents each. Orders over $5.00 are $0.75 per photo, orders under $5.00 are $1.00 per photo. Sorry, no stamps.

Phone: 212-691-7554

Grab Bag Hot Pics
c/o Freebird Publishers
221 Pearl St., Ste. 541
North Dighton, MA 02764

20 sexy photos for $13. Includes S/H with tracking. You choose the category; they choose the photos. All pictures are 4x6 glossy, non-nude. No duplicates in entire order. Choose from Asian, White, Latino, Black, Tattoo, Football Babes, Western Chicks, Cameltoe, Mixed Hotties Females and Mixed Hotties Males.

Send $13.00 per set ordered with info on paper. They are not responsible for mailroom refusals they give no

refunds, only credit vouchers less S/H costs. If want replacements, just have photos mailed back and $2.00 or 6 stamps with letter and they will gladly mail you new photos.

Hot Dreams
PO Box 192
Dequincy, LA 70633

"Get your new non-nude cat #31 and FREE photo. You must send a SASE along with 25 stamps or $6.00. Hundreds to choose in bikini and panties.

Get the non-nude super catalog package #1 that has over 2000 hot White babes in panties, lingerie and thongs. Your favorite types of shots only $15.00 FREE S/H. Comes with 5 FREE pictures.

By Mike Enemigo

To receive a 30 picture set of cameltoe shots and coeds of all sexy, hot White babes, send only $20.00 along with 4 stamps. They are hot. In panties, bras, thongs and G-strings.

Got stamps? Send 50 stamps to get 10 non-nude hot pictures. Send $20.00 to get non-nude catalogs 2-11. Comes with 5 FREE pictures.

Send $6.00 to get non-nude catalog #30.

Send only $15.00 to get the all nude big pack catalog #1. Has thousands to choose from. Comes with 5 FREE pictures."

Review: They definitely offer some great images. A lot of pussy shots. It looks like this company is either affiliated with FIYA Girls, or was bought out by them because they changed their address to theirs. – Mike

Hot Girl Safari
c/o Freebird Publishers
221 Pearl St., Ste. 541
North Dighton, MA 0264

This is a non-nude photo book. Full color gloss photos. A different photo on each page. Over $100.00 worth of sexy photos. The book is a soft cover, 8.3x6 inches, 128 pages. Send $24.99 plus $7.00 S/H with tracking.

Inmate-Connection.com
PO box 83897
Los Angeles, CA 90083

"Only the best and hottest photos. They have the newest, most sensational and exclusive photos on the planet. To order our FREE catalog, send SASE or $1.20. All photos are prison friendly. All photos are 4x6, high quality and glossy.

Photo prices:

- 12 photos for $10.00
- 16 photos for $15.00
- 22 photos for $20.00
- 28 photos for $25.00
- 35 photos for $30.00
- 45 photos for $35.00

Minimum order is $10.00 Additional pictures with any set are $.80 each. Add a flat rate of $2.20 for shipping on all orders. They will not ship your order without payment for postage. They do not accept stamps for payment. They have been in business since July 2002."

Review: Good images. -Mike

Inmate Photo Service
Box 245895
Sacramento, CA 95824

For $3 you receive 8 color pgs. 2 pgs. of CA girls. In fact, these girls get around a bit so these photos aren't sold in CA. Black, white and Asian girls, very nice. Also included are some greeting cards. Limited selection mostly Asian but they're looking for artists and will buy your art or trade.

Inmate Services
PO Box 535547
Grand Prairie, TX 75053

Color catalogs are $2.00 each, and that includes shipping and handling. 4x6 photos are $0.45 each, calendars $2.00 to $4.00

New Inmate Services Digest $12.00 each, 1-year subscriptions $30 (3 issues). Published 3 times a year, each issue approximately 30 pages, 5.5 x 8.5. Contains girls photo, inmate art, comic, reading materials and more.

"They make all photos on the spot and get them in the mail to you fast. They don't send your order off to third party photos makers, they own our own photo lab. They have been swapping out our denied photos with photos of our choice sent back with denial slip since January 1, 2010. Straight forward pricing and they don't charge extra for envelopes or dividing your photos up per your mailroom's rules. They believe you should get what you pay for. Don't get robbed by companies with low-quality photos, no customer service, no swap out policy, and long waiting periods."

Review: They sent me a few catalogs. 'K-Series Catalog #6' is good. It's 3 pages (6 sides) and has a lot of fine ladies. 'May 2015' and 'September 2015, also 3 pages (6 sides) each are OK. Typical whores. Nothing you'd kick out of bed (or even think about it), but not a good, in my opinion (and I'm an expert) as the 'K-Series Catalog #61. - Mike

Kenneth Passaro
18 Belmont Ave. #2
Haledon, NJ 07509-1799
"

They offers non nude photos, no kids, don't ask. Nothing obscene in photos, only one person per. $1 per photo with a 20 photo minimum order. He is here to help and won't do anything illegal or immoral. Accepts stamps, facility check and Paypal for payments. Send payments to Kenneth Passaro. For more info send invite on JPay.

Email: aorganization3@aol.com

Krasnya LLC
PO Box 32082
Baltimore, MD 21282

"Welcome to Krasnya Babes and Krasnya Studs World. Tens of thousands of the hottest and most scandalous babes and dudes found on the planet. Each catalog has 120 beautiful girls or boys posing just for you. Order one catalog page for only $4.50 or 10 U.S. Forever stamps with a SASE. They will send you volume one. Each additional volume is the same price. They are more than happy to answer email inquiries; however, due to mailing costs of $0.49 cents a letter, enclose a SASE with all inquiries sent through the mail. Otherwise, no replies. Prices and policies? Color prints on 4x6 glossy photo paper as low as $0.35 cents per print on orders over 500, shipped according to policy: 25 pictures shipped every 24 hours. S/H is $2.00 per envelope. Method of payment: U.S. Postal Service money orders or state and federal correctional checks made out only to Krasnya, LLC.

Send $24.95 for a grab bag of 50 photos. You specify race and main area of your interests, they will pick selection for you. They will also throw in a bonus catalog of 120 babes, nude or BOP-friendly.

Send 3 brand-new flat books of 20 U.S. Forever stamps for a grab bag of 45 photos. You specify race and main area of interest; they will pick selection. They will also throw in a bonus color catalog page of 120 babes of studs. Please include 6 First Class Forever with this order for S/H.

For Krasnya clients who work the yards, have they got a great deal for you... Mr. Hustle Grab Bag Bargain Days, only 250 per babe/print. 5 grab bag minimum purchase required. $2.00 S/H per bag. 25 awesome babes per bag at only $6.25. You must buy at least 5 grab bags for this deal. You may want to sit down for this bonus bargain... Their Babes catalog special of the decade. 5 color catalogs for $6; 10 color catalogs for $12; 15 color catalogs for $18; 20 color catalogs for $24. Their catalog special is available only when you purchase the 5 grab bag minimum. The price includes FREE shipping on the catalogs. Because of shipping terms, all catalogs sold in multiples of 5 for $6 only. You choose male or female, nude or non-nude.

Want a FREE sample catalog from Krasnya? Send a SASE with 2 First Class stamps. 120 babes in each catalog. You choose male or female, nude or non-nude."

Email: krasnyababes@hotmall.com

Madam Photo
221 Pearl St., Ste. 552
North Dighton, MA 02764
Phone: 774-406-8682 (text)

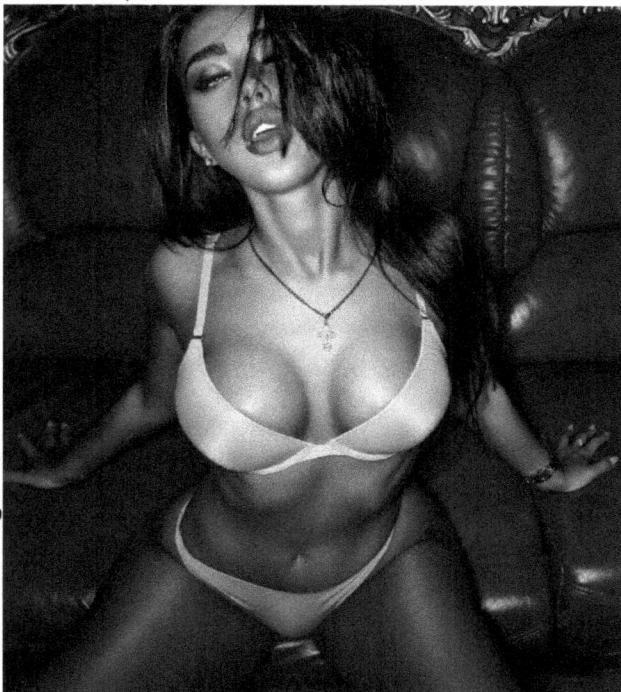

A sister company of Freebird Publishers that has been being created for the last couple years. Seller of non nude photo sets, female and male models, all which share their first name with you. The photo collections are Female Escort, Male Escort, Play-Girl, Play-Boy, Call Girl and Gigolo. Female collection models are separated into nationality and hair color. Male collection models are divided into bears, boys next door, muscle guys and swimmers. Photos sets have 5-8 and/or 9-12 photos per set. The choices do not stop there, difference photo finishes and sizes are offered for each too. Each photo set comes with an added Bonus. In addition you can order Designer Collage Posters available in any photo set and Designer Single Photo Posters available in any single photo from any photo set, posters come in different paper finishes and sizes. Madam Photo will also be offering speciality items personalized with a photo, to be send to you (if prison mail rooms allow) or for sending as a gift to someone on the outside, items like playing cards, puzzles, mugs, etc. Color Gloss catalog has over 500+ photos (more being added every month), one from each photo set for your ordering selections send $9.99 plus $4 for tracking. For more information see our advertisement on the back cover.

MoonLite Productions
PO Box 1304
Miami, FL 33265

"You've seen all those videos and TV shows that show you all the beautiful girls at South Beach, partying at the hottest clubs in Miami. Now you can see for yourself; let us show you just how hot the girls in Miami really are. They have a huge selection of hot, sexy girls showing off their beautiful bodies for you. We try our best to have something to please every taste.

Some companies sell poor quality pictures; some you can even tell they are taken from pages of magazines or posters. They offer excellent professional quality. They have girls wearing the smallest G-string bikinis, sexy outfits, lingerie, or spread nude. They also have pictures with penetration, and hot XXX action. They have whatever your institution allows. Make sure you know what you are allowed to receive. If any pictures they send you within the rules are rejected by the institution, they will exchange them when you send us a SASE and they get the originals back. If you have a question and write without an order, you MUST include a SASE or DO NOT expect a reply.

Half sets are 5 pictures for $7.49 or 25 stamps. Full sets are 10 4x6 pictures for $14.98 or 45 stamps. Get 15 pictures (a full set and a half) for $22 or 65 stamps. Get 20 pictures (2 full sets) for $29 or 85

stamps. Penetration/action sets are 8 for $14.98. Individual pictures are $1.50 each. Payment in stamps includes shipping. NO loose stamps please. Join our VIP Club and get FREE shipping on ALL orders while you are a member.

Sorry but they don't offer FREE samples. You can request a FREE catalog of almost 100 models when you send a $25 order or higher (not including shipping). If ordering less, then add $1.00 to get it. To order just the catalog send $1.50 or 5 stamps. They are always looking for hot new models to add, so there are more girls which do not appear in the catalog. They can make your first order a variety set of beautiful girls. Then you could tell us who you'd like to see more of, or if you want another variety set the next time. They have a high volume of sales. Some models are so popular that it's really hard to keep their pictures in stock. You can request your favorite models, but they reserve the right to substitute if they don't have pictures that would be allowed of the girls you ask for. They suggest you give us second and third choices just in case."

Shipping/Handling for pictures:

1-5 pictures: $1.00
6-10 pictures: $2.00
11-15 pictures: $3.00
16-20 pictures: $4.00, etc.
Order $100 or more and get FREE shipping

The Movie Market
Box 699
San Juan Capistrano, CA 92693

No longer prints catalogs but if you write, send SASE and ask they will send you a list of available photos, along with tiny photo of the celeb you requested. Photos are 4" x 6" and 8" x 10." High quality.

Phone: 949-488-8444
Web: moviemarket.com

Naughty Neighbot Pixx
PO Box 3074
Spring, TX 77383

They seem not to have any online presence or electronic contact. They offer sexy photos. Send 2 stamp SASE and get 2 free catalogs. Special 100 photos for $35.

Nickels and Dimez
14173 Northwest Fwy. 154
Houston, TX 77040

They offer color catalogs for $2 and B&W for $0.50 cents, 144 photos. Due to mail volume limit your letters to orders or checking order status. Always send a complete SASE or they will not respond.

Phone: 832-756-3377
Web: NickelsandDimez.com
Email: nickelsanddimez1@gmail.com

Nothing Butt Pictures
Inmate little Helpers
Box 4234
Oakland, CA 94614

This photo company is run and owned by Inmates' Little Help- ers. Offer many different categories of photos. To request catalog send SASE plus five First class stamps to cover printing costs. Offer Special 10 photo deal $6.75 in- house photos.

Web: InmatesLittleHelpers.com
Email: nothingbuttpictures@gmail.com

Nubian Princess Entertainment
PO Box 37
Timmonsville, SC 29161

Nubian Princess Entertainment is operated by porn star Chanail Paree. Know what you can receive before your order.

Each flier is $2.00 plus postage and handling. Fliers are all in black and white. (Photos, 4x6, are in full color.) There are no refunds or exchanges, so order carefully.

Fliers:

1. Short N Mini Skirt Flier: SM1-SM42; contains 42 very mild photos (a variety of pictures).
2. Short N Mini Skirt Flier: SM43-SM84; contains 42 very mild photos (a variety of pictures).
3. Short N Mini Skirt Flier: SM85-SM126; contains 42 very mild photos (a variety of pictures).
4. Short N Mini Skirt Flier: SM127-SM168; contains 42 very mild photos (pictures from Hawaii, car show & bike week).
5. Short N Mini Skirt Flier: SM169-SM210; contains 42 very mild photos (pictures from Hawaii, Adult Film Convention).
6. Short N Mini Skirt Flier: SM211-SM252; contains 42 very mild photos (lots of white hoes from an Adult Film Convention
7. Short N Mini Skirt Flier: SM253-SM294; contains 42 very mild photos (pictures mainly of Chanail, tight white pants and mini skirt).
8. Diva Selections Flier: D2S1-D2542; contains 42 mild/semi-hot photos (no thongs or girls bent over, but all back shots).
9. Diva Selections Flier: D2S43-D2S84; contains 42 mild/semi-hot photos (all front shots).
10. Sexy Divas Bikini Selections: S2D1-S2D42; contains 42 mild photos (bikini frontal pictures, Hawaiian/Philippine girls).
11. Hot Chicks Flier: HC1-HC42; contains 42 HOT mainly bike week photos (some back thong shots, mainly Chanail).
12. Hot Chicks Flier: HC43-HC84; contains 42 HOT pictures (a few back/thong shots/bent over from the AVN Porn Convention, lots of white hoes).
13. Hot Chicks Flier: HC85-HC1 26; contains 42 HOT back/thong/bent over shots (bike week pictures, variety of girls).
14. Nude Babes Flier: NB1-N842; contains 42 NUDE photos..
15. Nude Babes Flier: N843-NB84; contains 42 NUDE photos..
16. Nude Babes Flier: NB85-NB126; contains 42 NUDE and/or explicit photos (according to Jail standards)..

Each catalog is $5.00 plus postage and handling. Catalogs are all in black and white. All girls are in bikini/thong, and all shots are back shots or with legs wide open. They don't black out any parts of the catalog.

Catalogs:

- ✪ Catalog #1. C. Paree and Friends - Chanail with some Black hoes and a few white ones.
- ✪ Catalog #2. Myrtle Beach Bike Week, 120 photos - all Black girls.
- ✪ Catalog #3. Adult Magazine Models, 120 photos - Staring porn star Ayana Angel and other Black Tail/ big butt mag models.
- ✪ Catalog #4. Pictures from Vegas Stripper/Porn Star Convention, 125 photos, lots of white girls..
- ✪ Catalog #5. C Paree only, 120 photos - just me from lots of various locations -Tons..
- ✪ Catalog #6. Chanail and Friends, 140 mouth-watering NUDE photos..
- ✪ Catalog #7. Top Models, 126 photos - hot porn stars and more. Famous names, white Spanish and Black.

Postage & Handling:

If your order costs $2.00 - $5.99, add/supply a SASE with 2 current rate stamps on the envelope. If you need multiple envelopes, it's $2.00 per envelope, or $2.80 per envelope with confirmation.

If your order costs $6.00 - $15.00, add $2.00. If your order costs $15.01 - $20.00, add $3.00.

If you order costs $20.01 or more, add $3.40.

They strongly recommend that you send all of your merchandise with confirmation delivery. That will be $2.80 for each additional envelope that you need. They also strongly recommend that you do not order more than 3 fliers or 2 catalogs at a time since the prisons have a lot of crazy rules. This will prevent items from returning – less headaches for both of us. Please allow up to 6 weeks for delivery. If your order returns to us, they'll be happy to send it to an outside source, but its $4.00 to forward returned packages. For more info, or if you have any questions, send SASE.

Package Trust
370 W. Pleasantview Ave., Ste. #303
Hackensack, NJ 07601

Package Trust is powered by Don Diva.

"Send $7.00 for our full-color catalog of services and over 500 available sexy, non-nude photos. They sell our photos for $1.00 each.

If you would like a return response from Package Trust, you MUST send a SASE."

Phone Number: 347-815-3229
Email: packagetrust@dondivamag.com

Pantee Publishing LLC
PO Box 233
Hawthorne, NJ 07507

Offer nude and non nude photos. Send for more information.

Hot Deals, after four orders of $27.50 or higher get one free (must be same or equal amount in all four times). Minium orders is 10 photos for $11.50.
25 photos plus 5 free for $27.50 a total of 30 photos in all!

Bundle Deals
50 photos $45.00, 60 photos $50.00, 85 photos plus 3 catalogs $70.00 and 120 photos plus 4 catalogs $90.00.

Catalogs choices, all come in nude and non nude.
Ebony, White, Latina, Asian, Indian, Hardcore XXX, Busty, Big Booty, BBW, Milf, Celeb (non nude), Midget.

We no longer offer catalog photo orders as of 2018. If you would like a return response from you MUST send a SASE.

Phone Number: 347-815-3229
Email: packagetrust@dondivamag.com

Pillow Talk
c/o Freebird Publishers
221 Pearl St., Ste. 541
North Dighton, MA 0264

Non nude photos book. These attractive and sexy girls will keep you company at any time of day. They will pick you up in the mornings and put some pep in your step in the afternoons. For when the long evenings come around these beauties are at their best with pillow talk. Full color gloss non-nude photos. A different photo on every page. Over $100+ worth of sexy photos in one book, for one low price. Non-nude prison friendly. Softcover, 8.25 x 5.25", 150+ pages. Send $24.99 plus $7.00 S/H with tracking.

Prison L S
Box 686
Eustace, TX 75124

They offer non nude photos sets and specific catalog photos picks. Have monthly photosets, female named sets, and photos that can be purchased from catalogs. Photo set prices range from $40-$200. Catalogs have 800 photos on four pages front and back prices from $4-$10. In addition, they offer Add Money To Inmate Account from $50-$300 and a Parole Package for $400 marked down from $500.

Photo: 430-808-3228
Web: prisonls.com
Email: help@prisonls.com

R. Hughson
Box 1033
Neenah, WI 54957

Offer a high quality photos with super-fast shipping. Also offer a wide variety of services other than just photos. Send SASE for updated information.

Ruby Red Entertainment
Box 155
Covington, VA 24426

New to the market. Started by ex-inmate. The self-published Tru Royalty Magazine is about street life in VA, NY and more. 100 pages, color, 8.5" x 11". Due to the content and this not being a prisoner magazine, be careful of mailroom rejection. Start with the single issue just in case. Single issues are $10 and a yearly subscription which is four issues is $35, printed quarterly.

Phone: 571-255-5119
Web: rubyredentertainment.com

Email: admin@rubyredentertainment.com

South Beach Singles, Inc.
PO Box 1656
Miami, FL 33238

All photos are $1.00 each with a minimum order of 10 photos per brochure, plus a flat rate of $3.00 S/H. They offer a special - 30 photos for $20.00. You can get 10 photos for 40 stamps (flat books only).

Brochure lists, non-nude, $2.00 each:

NBA Vol. 9: White, everyday women, amateurs, open legs and backshots.

NBA Vol. 10-13: Black women, strippers, amateurs, open legs, backshots. Some White girls here - Sasha Cream, Cubana Lust (Cubana), and Amber (Vol. 12).

NBA Vol. 14-17: Nix of Black, White, action shots and adult stars.

Brochure lists, XXX, $5.00 each:

Triple XXX Vol. 1: Pinky, Cherokee, Luscious Lopez, Olivia, Sky and Mason.

Triple XXX Vol. 2: Montana Fishburne, Next Door Nikki, Flower, Phoenix, Jadalsis, Angel, Kapri, more Pinky and Cherokee.

Triple XXX Vol. 3: Lacey, Misty, Mika, Kelly, Pleasure, Pinky and Cherokee.

Custom orders are 25 photos for $40 (S/H included): "I will allow you to choose from your favorite model, adult star, or celebrity of your choice. Send $40 along with your feature and I will send you 25 of the hottest photos I can find. The custom will also apply to fetishes. Also Instagram and Facebook photos you want me to find. You must have the specific Instagram or Facebook user name they are using. I will not search for it. Please keep in mind this is a VIP service; you are getting photos that no one else has. Most celebrities and models will NOT have action shots, but I will get you the best high-quality photos no company can match. (Sorry, no transgender.) Please allow 10 days for delivery."
Karen Leblanc, CEO

Email/Corrlinks: rd@southbeachsingles.org
Website: southbeachsingles.org

The Senza Collection
PO Box 5840
Baltimore, MD 21282

Senza specializes in providing you several choices -all-nude 4x6 prints in startling vivid color imagery, or non-nude 4x6 prints in startling vivid color imagery.

They have divided our catalogs into these categories: Caucasian, African-American, Hispanic, Asian, and Mixed Hotties. Each page of our catalogs has 99 gloriously seductive ladies posing just for your enjoyment.

By Mike Enemigo

There are over 250 catalogs to collect at just $2.50 per catalog. You can order a FREE "99 Hotties" sample catalog by sending 2 First Class Forever stamps and a SASE.

For those that just cannot wait, take advantage of our introductory special - Dirty Dozen. $19.99 gets you all of this, plus FREE S/H: 12 eye-popping catalogs, each with 99 pictures to choose from, and 12 - 4x6 random prints from our Mixed Hotties selection to show off our 4x6 print quality. All for just $19.99.

Remember, you must specify nude or non-nude, as well as your institution's restrictions as to the number of prints allowed in one envelope.

Please review our policies carefully: All Senza images are sold at a flat rate of $0.35 cents each. Anyone wishing to purchase 1000 plus prints at one time will be given a flat rate of $0.30 cents per image. They have a minimum requirement of $15.00, which doesn't include S/H charges.

S/H charges are as follows:

- ✪ 1-5 4x6 prints: $1.00 per envelope
- ✪ 6-15 4x6 prints: $1.50 per envelope
- ✪ 16-25 4x6 prints: $2.00 per envelope

You must notify us on the order form the amount of prints your institution will allow in each envelope. They will accept brand-new US First Class postage stamps at the rate of $5.00 per book of 20. You are required to know your institution's policies regarding what images are acceptable into your facility. There are no exceptions to this policy. Returned/rejected mail: You will have 15 business days to send us a SASE (3 stamps per 25 rejected photos) with a street address in which to mail your returned/rejected photos. After 15 days the prints will return to our inventory. All sales are final, no refunds or exchanges.

Sexy Girl Parade
c/o Freebird Publishers
221 Pearl St., Ste. 541
North Dighton, MA 0264

This is a non-nude photo book. Full color gloss photos. A different photo on each page. Over $100.00 worth of sexy photos. The book is a soft cover, 8.3x6 inches, 124 pages. Send $24.99 plus $7.00 S/H with tracking.

SJE Photos
PO Box 50
Alvarado, TX 76009

They sell non nude photos. Catalog prices: two stamps per catalog and one SASE per four catalogs. Catalogs, are one page, two sided with 70 images per catalog. Catalogs available in color or B&W. Six catalogs released every 30 days. Photos are priced $0.70 each 4" x 6", $2 each 5" x 7", $5 per 8" x 10" with free S/H. They offer exchanges with return of denied photos and SASE. They offer inmate house accounts. They only offer photos, nothing else.

Soft Shots
c/o Freebird Publishers
221 Pearl St., Ste. 541
North Dighton, MA 0264

Come see our beautiful ladies dressed in the tiniest of outfits and posing in many different alluring positions. This is a non-nude photo book. Full color gloss photos. A different photo on each page. Come see our beautiful ladies dressed in the tiniest of outfits and posing in many different alluring positions. Full color gloss non-nude photos.

Surrogate Sisters
PO Box 95043
Las Vegas, NV 89193

They sell non-nude photos. Minimum order is 5 photos.
Five photos: $9.00 or 25 new Forever stamps.
10 photos: $15.00 or 45 new Forever stamps.

Their fliers are $2.00 or 5 Forever stamps each. W = White. H = Hispanic, B = Black, and A = Asian. There is no difference between SS and VIP fliers other than to help you/us identify. When ordering fliers, write down the specific number/ name/etc.

Here are our current catalogs:

SS1: H, W, Girls; front and side shots.
S52: H. W, girls; front and back shots.
SS3: W, H girls; front and back shots.
SS4: H, W girls; front, back and side shots.
SS5: W, B girls; front, back and side shots.
SS6: H, B girls; front back and side shots.
SS7: H, B girls; front and back shots.
SS8: B, H, W girls; use name.
SS9: H, A, W girls; use name.
SS10: W girls, many poses; use name.
SS11: W girls, many poses; use name.
SS12: W girls, many poses; use name.
SS13: B girls, many poses.
SS14: B, W girls; use name.
SS15: W, A, B girls; use name.
S516: B, W, A girls; front and back shots.
SS17: B, W, A girls; front and back shots.
SS18: B, W, A girls; some 2 girls.
SS19: B, W, A girls; front and back shots.
SS20: B, W girls; some 2 girls.
SS21: H, W girls; front and back shots.
SS22: B girl, mostly front shots.
SS23: B girl, in house and by the pool.
SS24: H. W girls, on bike and Hummer.
SS25: H, W girls, on bike and Hummer.
SS26: H, W, B girls on bikes and cars.
SS27: H, W girls on bikes.
SS28: H, W girls, many poses all over.
SS29: H, W girls, on bikes, cars, trucks.
SS30: W girls, bikini front shots.
SS31: B, W girls, bikini back shots.
SS32: B girls, back and side shots.
SS33: B girls, back shots.
SS34: B, W girls, some 2 girls.
SS35: W girls, some 2 girls.
SS36: B girl, many poses in home.
SS37: W girl, many poses in home.
SS38: B, W girls, frontal shots.
SS39: B girls, front and back shots.
SS40: A, W girls, poses on a soft rug.
SS41: H girl, Latino spice, many poses.
SS42: B, W girls, mostly back shots.
SS43: W girls, some 2 girls.

SS44: B, W girls, some 2 girls.
SS45: B girl, many poses in home.
SS46: B, H girls, in home and by Lexus.
SS47: B, W, H girls, chunky shots.
SS48: B girl, in home and by Lexus.
SS49: B, W girls, chunky.
SS50: Cars, Ice Cube, some girls.
SS52: W, B girls, many poses.
SS53: B girls, some in Lexus.
SS54: B girl, in home and limo.
SS55: B, W girls, many in home.
SS56: W girls, many poses in home.
SS57: W, B girls, many in home.
SS58: W, B girls, many poses in home.
SS59: W, B girls, many poses in home.
SS60: H girls, many poses in home.
SS6I: H girls, many poses.
SS62: H girls, many poses.
SS63: H girls, many poses.
SS64: B girls, many poses in home.
SS65: B girls, many poses in home.
SS66: B girls, front and back shots.
SS67: B girls, front and back shots.
SS68: B girls, front and back shots.
SS69: Men, W and H.
SS70: Men, W, H and B.
SS71: Men, W and B.
SS72: Men, W and H.
SS73: Men, W and H.
SS74: Pregnant girls.
SS75: Pregnant girls.
SS76: Redheaded girls.
SS77: Redheaded girls.
SS78: Chunky girls.
SS79: Chunky girls.
SS80: Chunky girls.
SS81: Girls fully clothed.
SS82: Girls fully clothed.
SS83: W, H girls, 2 or more.
SS84: W, H girls, 3 or more.
SS85: W, H girls, 2 or more.
SS86: W, H girls, 2 or more.
SS87: W, H girls, 2 or more.

By Mike Enemigo

SS88: H girls, front and side shots.
SS89: H girls, front and side shots.
SS90: H girls, all poses.
SS91 H girls, all poses.
SS92: H, W, A girls, various poses.
SS93: W girls, wet in shower.
SS94: W, H girls, back shots.
SS95: W, H girls, back shots.
SS96: W, H girls, back shots.
SS97: W, H girls, back shots.
SS98: W, H girls, back shots.
SS99: W, H girls, back shots.
SS100: W girls, bikini, front shots.
SS101: W girls, bikini shots.
SS102: W girls, front and back.
SS103: B girls, front and back.
SS104: B girls, back shots.
SS105: W, B, H, a girls' foot show.
SSI06: W girls all wet.
SS107: W girls, topless/covered.
SS108: W girls, front and side shots.
SS109: W girls in lingerie.
SSI10: W gothic girls.
SS111: W gothic girls.
SS112: W gothic girls.
SSI13: W gothic girls.
SS114: Men.
SS115: Men.
SS116: Men.
SSI17: Men.
SS118: Men.
SS119: W girls.
SS120: W girls.
SS121: W girls.
SS122: W girls.
SS123: W girls.
SS124: W girls.
SS125: W, H girls.

SS126: W girls.
SS127: A girls.
SS128: A girls.
SS129: A girls.
SS130: A girls.
SS131: A girls.
SS132: A girls.
SS133: A girls.
SS134: A girls.
SS135: A girls.
SS136: W, H, B, A girls' feet.
SS137: W, B, H girls' feet show.
SS138: W, B, H girls' feet show.
SS139: W, H, a girl's foot show.
SS140: B girls; front, side and back.
SS141: B girls; front, side and back.
SS142: B girls, front and back.
SS143: B girls, front and side shots.
SS144: B girls, front and side shots.
SS145: B girls, front and side shots.
SS146: W, H girls with tattoos.
SS147: Transsexual photos.
SS148: W, H girls; cameltoe.
SS149: Girls in sexy costumes.
SS150: Girls in sexy costumes.
SS151: Girls in sexy costumes.
SS152: Girls in sexy costumes.
SS153: Girls in sexy costumes.
SS154: Girls in sexy costumes.
SS155: Girls in sexy costumes.
SS156: Girls in sexy costumes.
SS157: Girls In sexy costumes.
SS158: Girls in sexy costumes.
SS159: W, H girls, front and side.
SS160: W, H girls, front and side.
SS161: H girls; front, side and back.
SS162: H girls; front, back and side.
SS163: W, H girls, front and back.

Kitty Kat: Adult Entertainment Non Nude Resource Book

SS164: W, H girls, front and side.
SS165: W, H girls, front and side.
SS166: W, H girls, front and back.
SS167: W, H girls, front and back.
SS168: W, H girls, front and back.
SS169: W, H girls, front and back.
SS170: W, H girls, front and back.
SS17I: W, H girls, front and back.
SS172: W, H girls, front and back.
SS173: W, H, A girls, front and side.
SS174: W girls, sexy stockings.
SS175: W girls, sexy stockings.
SS176: W girls, sexy stockings.
SS177: W, B, H midget girls.
SS178: W, H big and busty girls.
SS179: W, H, B big and busty girls.
SS180: W, H, big and busty girls.
SS181: W, H, big and busty girls.
SS182: W, H, big and busty girls.
SS183: W, H, big and busty girls.
SS184: W, H, big and busty girls.
SS185: W, H, big and busty girls.
SS186: W, H, B girls; front shots.
SS187: W, H, B, various girls.
SS188: W, H, sexy office girls.
SS189: W, H, sexy office girls.
SS190: W, H, college party girls.
SS191: W, H, A college girls.
SS192: W, H, college party girls.
SS193: W, H, college parts girls.
SS194: W, H, college party girls.
SS195: W, H, college party girls.
SS196: W, H, college party girls.
SS197: W, H girls with feet.
SS198: W bikini models.
SS199: W bikini models.
SS200: W bikini models.
VIP1: B girl in home and by Lexus.
VIP2: B girl, many poses in home.
VIP3: B, H girls, in home and by Lexus.
VIP4: B, H, W girls, many poses.
VIP5: B, W girls; some 2 girls.
VIP6: W girls, some 2 girls.
VIP7: W girls, by bikes and cars.
VIP8: W, H girls, on bikes and Lexus.
VIP9: W, H girls, poses in home.
VIP10: W, H girls, poses in home.
VIP11: W, H girls, in home and garden.
VIP12: W girls, some 2 girls.
VIP13: H girls, many spreading poses.
VIP14: H girls, many poses in home.
VIP15: H girls, spreading poses.
VIP16: H girls, many poses in home.
VIP17: H girl, many poses.
VIP18: H girls, many spreading poses.
VIP19: W girls, many 2 girls.
VIP20: B girl by Christmas tree.
VIP21: B girl, many poses in home.
VIP22: W girls, bikini poses.

VIP23: W girls, bikini poses.
VIP24: W girls, bikini poses.
VIP25: W girls, bikini poses.
VIP26: W girls, bikini poses.
VIP27: W girls, bikini poses.
VIP28: W, B girls.
VIP29: W, A, sexy celebrity girls.
VIP30: W, A, sexy celebrity girls.
VIP31: W, A, B, sexy celebrity girls.
VIP32: A back shots.
VIP33: A back shots.
VIP34: A, W, front and back shots.
VIP35: W, A, many poses.
VIP36: A, W, mostly back shots.
VIP37: A back shots.
VIP38: A back shots.
VIP39: W, H, B girls, big butts.
VIP40: W, H girls, butts only.
VIP41: W girls, big breasts only.
VIP42: W girls, big breasts only.
VIP43: W girls, butts only.
VIP44: W girls, 2 or more.
VIP45: W mature women.
V1P46: W mature women.
VIP47: W mature women.
VIP48: W girls, many poses.
VIP49: W girls, feet only.
VIP50: W girls, many poses.
VIP51: W, it girls, many poses.
VIP52: W, it girls, many poses.
VIP53: W girls, mostly back shots.
VIP54: W girls, many poses.
VIP55: W girls, many poses.

By Mike Enemigo

VIP56: W, H girls, many poses.
VIP57: W girls, many poses.
VIP58: W, I-i girls, many poses.
VIP59: W girls, many poses.
VIP60: W girls, many poses.
VIP61: W, H girls, many poses.
VIP62: W, I-I girls, many poses.
VIP63: W girls, many poses.
VIP64: W girls, many poses.
VIP65: W girls, mostly back shots.
VIP66: W girls, mostly back shots.
VIP67: Fully clothed girls.
VIP68: Fully clothed girls.
VIP69: W girls, holiday and at sea.
VIP70: W mature women.
VIP71: W mature women.
VIP72: W older women.
VIP73: W mature women.
VIP74: W, B, H women, many poses.
VIP75: W girls, many poses.
VIP76: B, W, A muscle girls.
VIP77: W muscle girls.
VIP78: Female celebrities.

VIP79: Female celebrities.
VIP80: W gothic girls.
VIP81: W gothic girls.
VIP82: W swimsuit models.
VIP83: W swimsuit models.
VIP84: W swimsuit/lingerie models.
VIP85: W mature women.
VIP86: W mature women.
VIP87: W mature women.
VIP88: W, B lingerie models.
VIP89: W swimsuit models.
VIP90: W girls, many poses.
VIP91: W, H, shirtless males.
VIP92: W, B, shirtless males.
VIP93: W girls, 2 or more.
VIP94: W girls, 2 or more.
VIP95: W girls, 2 or more.
VIP96: A girls, back and side shots.
VIP97: A girls, back and side shots.
VIP98: A girls, back and side shots.
VIP99: A girls, back and side shots.
VIP100: A girls, back and side shots.

TRACKING: If you wish to have your order sent with a USPS tracking number, add $4.00 or 10 Forever stamps per envelope. SPECIAL: Any orders of $50.00 or more that are paid for with a check or money order will get all photos and/or fliers for $1 each. Send SASE for more info.

Website: surrogatesisters.com
Corrlinks: service@surrogatesisters.com

Top Notch Inmate Services
PO Box 268
Little Chute, WI 54140
topnotchinmatesvs@yahoo.com
This business is run by Christy Weiss, which worked for Elite Paralegal Services for years. They offer adult XXX stories and non nude erotic photos. For more info send SASE.

Total Access Services
PO Box 31764
Capitol Heights, MD 20731

All photos are $1 each and there is a 5 photo minimum per order. 30 photos for $20, 10 photos for 40 stamps (flat books only). Tell us how many photos your facility will allow per envelope. They are not responsible for rejected photos, but will replace up to 5.

Review: The quality of the catalog is ratchet, but the images they offer are cool. - Mike

Villa Entertainment Company, Inc.
14173 NW Freeway, Ste. 203
Houston, TX 77040

"Like the beautiful women on the pages of StreetSeen Magazine and the car shows they attend? Order 4x6 glossy photos of them. $12.00 for 10 photos of random 4x6 glossy premium non-nude photos of car show hotties. Catalog $3. Add $3.00 S/H for each envelope you need to have your pictures sent in. Hottest ladies in the car show scene are now available on posters, 11x17 $5 each plus $3 S/H. They are not responsible for rejected pictures."

S.T.O.P : Start Thinking Outside Prison
Inspiring Motivating Self-Help

Regain Your Power Beyond Prison Walls

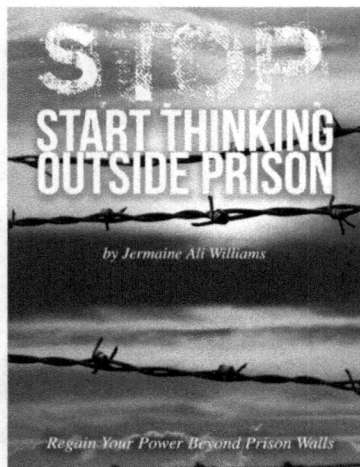

Greatness lies within many of my brothers and sisters. The problem is we tend to find ourselves incarcerated before we discover this greatness. Our thought patterns and consistent inability to think on a positive level leads us straight to prison.

Thinking is very critical to one's success, failure, and survival. Every decision requires thinking. If not, many actions will be done on impulse. And impulsive behavior tends to bring about situations from which one needs to be rescued. Think of a preteen, teenager, or young adult, all of whom can possess the impulsive behaviors of children. If the impulses aren't tamed or controlled, the behavior patterns will be present in each stage of life. Maybe this is the reason I see so many 40-year-olds that lack self-control or the ability to deal with some of life's simplest problems. They can't attack the situations from a professional, calm, and diplomatic standpoint.

S.T.O.P. was written as a movement to help promote a greater thinking process - a thinking process I believe will slow down the recidivism rate within our communities. This will mean that more fathers will be available in the household, more parents around to pass down the guidance that will enable our young boys to become men. Men who will stand accountable for the direction of their community.

As a man, I ask all men to join together and help rebuild what many of us helped destroy. It starts with you. It starts with me. No outside force can aid this cause until the aid is given from within. A better future is literally in our hands. It is my intent that the following ten chapters will provide enlightenment and force all of us to S.T.O.P. - Start Thinking Outside Prison!

Softcover, 6" x 9", 70+ Pgs., B&W Interior

Ask. Believe. Receive.
Our Power to Create Our Own Destiny

In life, true strength comes from never letting an experience define you. There is always a reason for everything – steppingstones on a path to better destinations.

Our words have immense creative power and determine where our paths will lead us. If we put positive words into the world we create reality from with them.

"Positive, creative and powerful," is how the Bible says we were created, and it explains the capabilities we all possess from birth.

We are gods – creators. We create our destiny with our words ... good or bad ... and we are responsible. Of course, that means that we are always capable of changing the course of our lives, by speaking good words.

This book will literally change your life and hopefully open your eyes to your own creative power.

A must-read for everyone!

A man's future consists of the faith inside of him. Whatever that faith is, so shall it become his reality. – The Bhagavagita

Softcover, 6" x 9", 92 Pgs., B&W Interior

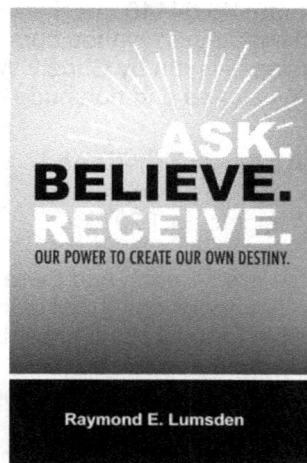

HOT GIRL SAFARI

Non Nude Photo Book

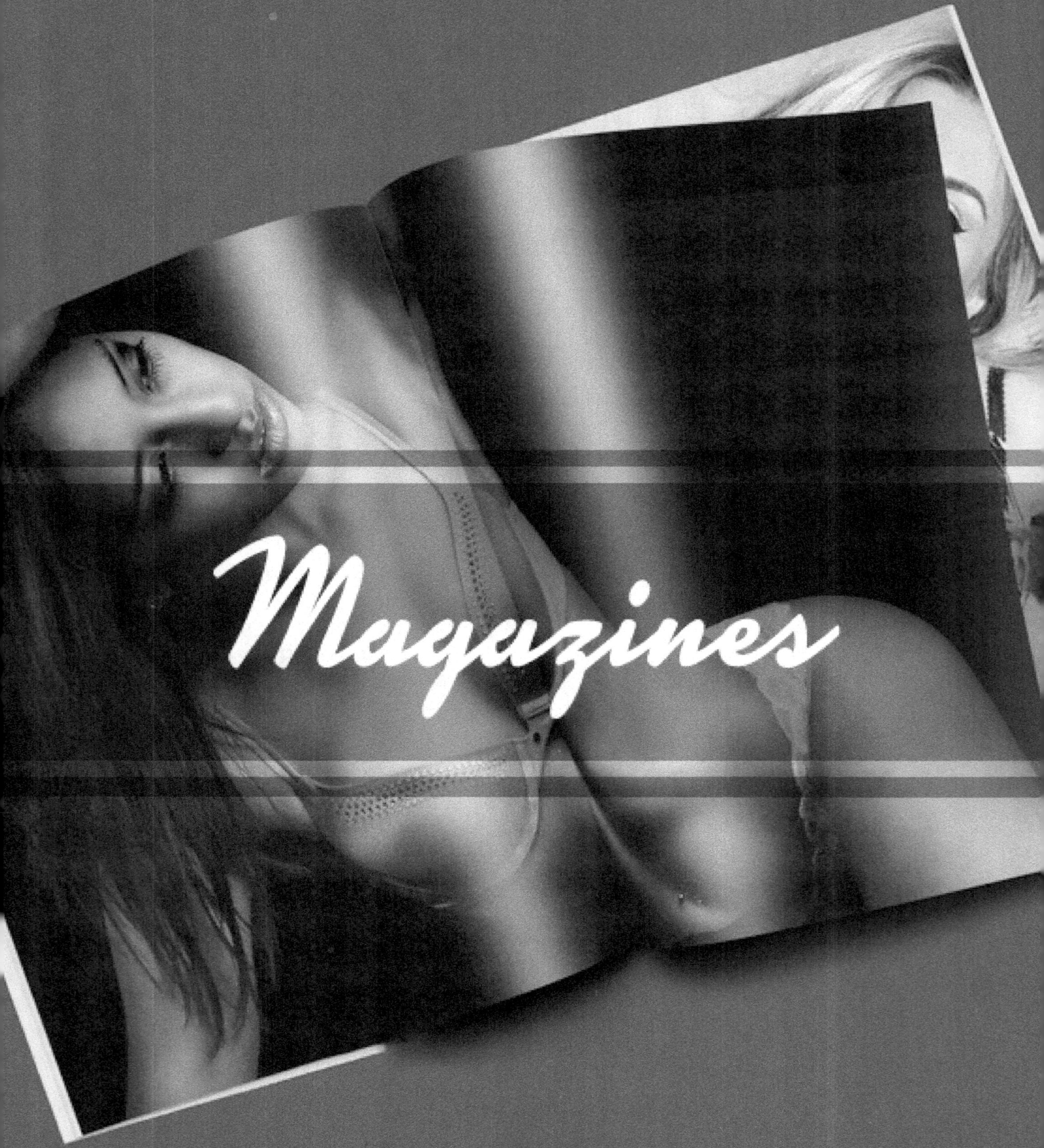
Magazines

MAGAZINES

The Art of Sexy
c/o Cummings Media
PO Box 9867
Ft. Lauderdale, FL 33310-9867

The Art of Sexy, by SHOW, is an all-nude magazine. Same hoes. $9.95 an issue, $34.95 for 4 issues, $54.95 for 8 issues. Add $6.95 for shipping and handling. For faster service log onto http://www.showgirlzexclusive.com.

Assets
c/o AS IS Magazine
1202 Lexington Ave., Ste. 317
New York, N.Y. 10028

"Welcome to Assets. Real quality, real models... That's what we're about. Black and white is not an issue in Assets. For us, beauty is but one color... PINK." Shabazz

Assets is brought to you by the urban/street magazine AS IS. It's full of bad babes. One-year subscription is only $36.00. It's a quarterly publication. They are not responsible for deliveries received by correctional facilities and not given to inmates. There will be no refunds. For an additional $2.00 per issue ($8.00 total) charge you can receive certified confirmation (optional).

Website: asismagazine.com

BlackMen Publications, Inc.

210 Route 4 East
Paramus, NJ 07652

100 plus pages of fine girls - urban models, mostly, thick and curvy. It's published bi-monthly. Yearly subscription (6 issues) is $29.00.

Review: I usually have a subscription to this magazine. Beautiful girls; Draya, Tahiry, Jesikah Maximus, Coco, Tatted Up Holly, Cubana Lust, etc.

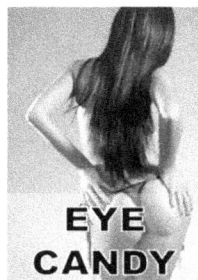

Eye Candy Magazine
c/o Inmate Service Corp.
441 Walina St. Ste. 408
Honolulu, HI 96815

www.iexmagazine.com
iexmanager47@gmail.com

ISC Eye Candy Magazine new issue due out mid of April. For those not familiar with the ISC they publish a magazine formatted towards the inmate population. It provides many scantily clad women for their visual appetite, exotic stories for their reading pleasure, legal news for their legal rights, and sports information for their gaming needs. Magazine Full Color, Gloss, 8.5 x 11", 100 pages. Subscriptions 6 Issues Yearly for $29.99.

I' Adore

c/o Rhymes & Dimes Publications
PO Box 138
Yonkers, NY 10705

I'ADORE is full of bad babes, and even has a couple of erotic stories - at least from the issue I've reviewed. Each issue is $14.99, shipping and handling included. Please allow 7 business days on all shipped orders. Rhymes & Dimes Publications is not responsible for any confiscated books by correctional facility. Rhymes & Dimes Publications, 'Where entertainment meets sexy,' also publishes Thick, Black Ink, and Rhymes & Dimes magazines. Each is $14.99.

Phat Puffs Magazine

c/o SUB 0 Entertainment, Inc.
PO Box 1222
New York, N.Y. 10029

Website: sub0world.com

"They designed the magazine to bring you the REAL. This mag brings you what's REALLY happening in the streets. They provide REAL woman, REAL interviews, with REAL answers, REAL events and REAL articles.. Let's keep it real; fans buy these magazines not only to see PHAT, BEAUTIFUL MODELS, but also to be entertained via HOT, SEXY, sensual positions, steamy HOT INTERVIEWS, etc. - not only to get excited, but in hopes of getting familiar with such women. As men, they want to learn how women think. In short, they want to get an understanding and edge on such confusing creatures. This magazine is designed to do just that. The babes in this mag are mostly strippers etc.. It's non-nude, but laid out very similar to a porn mag in style, and the pictures are about as close to porn you can get while remaining non-nude. Each issue is $9.99, plus $5.00 shipping and handling.

SB Studios

SUMMERBUNNIES
P.O. Box 741145
Houston, TX 77274

www.summerbunnies.com

SB Studios has been in business since 2002. They publish a non-nude magazine of premier ethnic bikini models as well as collectors trading cards.

Summer Bunnies Magazine Collectors Edition Intro Issue $13. 20 Pack of Trading Cards $12. (shipping and handling is included)

Cashier's checks or money orders accepted only (no stamps)

SHOW

c/o Cummings Media
PO Box 9867
Ft. Lauderdale, FL 33310-9867

SHOW is published bi-monthly by Cummings Media Inc. Single copy price is $9.95. Subscription price is $24.95 for six issues. Please add $6.95 for shipping and handling. For faster service have your people log onto show-mag.com or call 1-877-651-2819.

SHOW: Black Lingerie
PO Box 9867
Ft. Lauderdale, FL 33310-9867

SMOOTH Magazine
PO Box 809
New York, NY 10013-0803

SMOOTH Magazine contains "The Right Moves for Today's Man." It's a magazine full of beautiful urban models, articles, etc. They sell posters, calendars, back issues and a sub-magazine titled "SMOOTH Girl." You can write, vote for their hottest 100 SMOOTH girls of the year and more. The beautiful Ayisha Diaz is a contributing writer. A yearly subscription is $34.95.

Review: I usually have a subscription to this magazine. It has all the baddest models - Ayisha Diaz, Too Much Rosey, Yolie, Blac China, Maliah and more. There are interviews with the models so you can get to know them a little bit, and there are interesting articles, too. - Mike

Special Needs X-Press
927 Old Nepperhan Ave.
Yonkers, NY 10703
PH: 914-623-7007

Ships direct to any correctional facility. Offering a wide variety of
magazines. Loved ones can add money to an Inmate Account
with SNX.

StreetSeen Magazine & Car Show Hotties Magazine
c/o Villa Entertainment Co.
14173 NW Freeway, Ste. 203
Houston, TX 77040
PH: 713-465-9599
www.streetseen.com
streetseen@ymail.com

These magazines are filled with the hottest REAL girls in the scene.
Many exclusive, never before seen images from our archives. It's a must have collector's items! Limited run
editions. Car Show Hotties NOT available in stores. All Volumes now available! Magazines Full Color, Gloss,
8.5 x 11", 75-100 pages. StreetSeen Magazine $7.95 plus $3 S/H, Car Show Hotties $11.95 plus $3 S/H.
Offer non nude facility friendly.

Wall Periodicals
PO Box 2584
Plainfield, NJ 07060

Phone 718-819-1693 / 866-756-1370

www.WallPeriodicalsonline.com

Wall Periodicals is the largest urban magazine store. Order your single and back issues today.

- ✪ 504 DYMES
- ✪ ART OF SEXY
- ✪ ASSETS
- ✪ BARE ARMS
- ✪ BLACK MEN
- ✪ BODY
- ✪ BONITA
- ✪ BOTTLES & MODELZ
- ✪ CRAZE
- ✪ DAMN GIRL
- ✪ DIME PIECE
- ✪ HUSTLENOMICS
- ✪ I'ADORE
- ✪ KING
- ✪ MAXIM
- ✪ ORIGINATORS
- ✪ PHAT PUFFS
- ✪ POLE
- ✪ RHYMES & DIMES
- ✪ SHOW
- ✪ SHOW BLACK LINGERIE
- ✪ SHY GIRL
- ✪ SKIN TONES
- ✪ SMOOTH
- ✪ SMOOTH GIRL

- ✪ SPICY
- ✪ SI SWIMSUIT EDITION
- ✪ STACK
- ✪ STUNNAZ
- ✪ STRAIGHT STUNTIN
- ✪ SWEETS
- ✪ THICK
- ✪ TRAP INK
- ✪ UHM AND MORE..

Send SASE today for a FREE
catalog..

By Mike Enemigo

QUINN
Playgirl Collection
White

Madam Photo
PRESENTS

FLETCHER
Play-Boy Collection
Boy Next Door

MACY
Female Escort Collection
Black

Madam
Photo
A FREEBIRD PUBLISHERS
COMPANY

FELICITY
Female Escort Collection
White

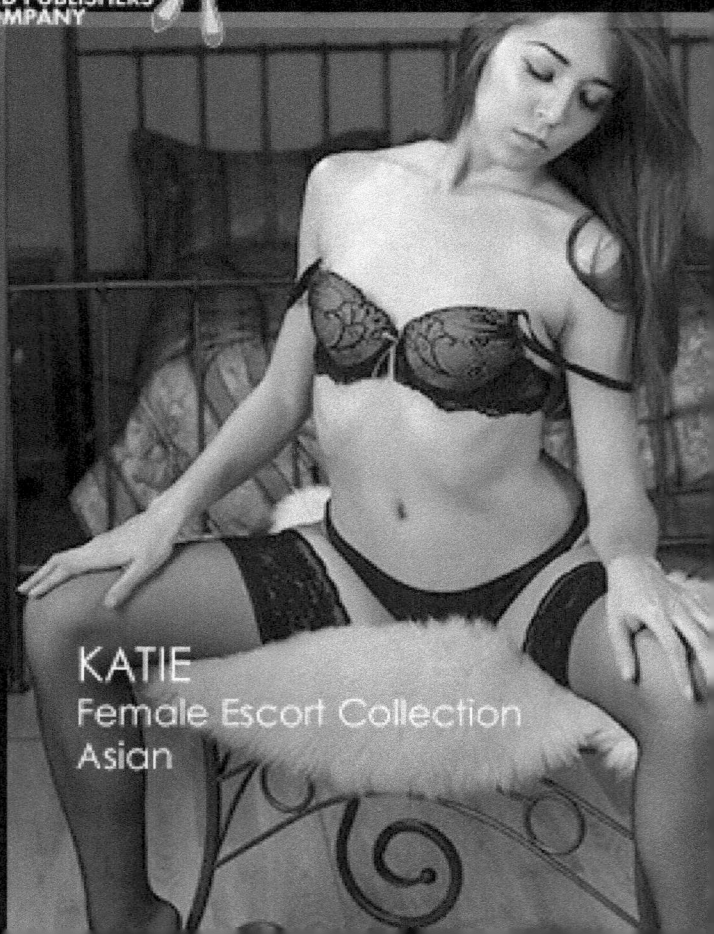

KATIE
Female Escort Collection
Asian

Madam Photo
A FREEBIRD PUBLISHERS COMPANY

QUINN
Playgirl Collection
White

TRISTAN
Male Escort Collection
Boy Next Door

LAITH
Play-Boy Collection
Bear

ISAAC
Male Escort Collection
Muscle

Madam
Photo
A FREEBIRD PUBLISHERS

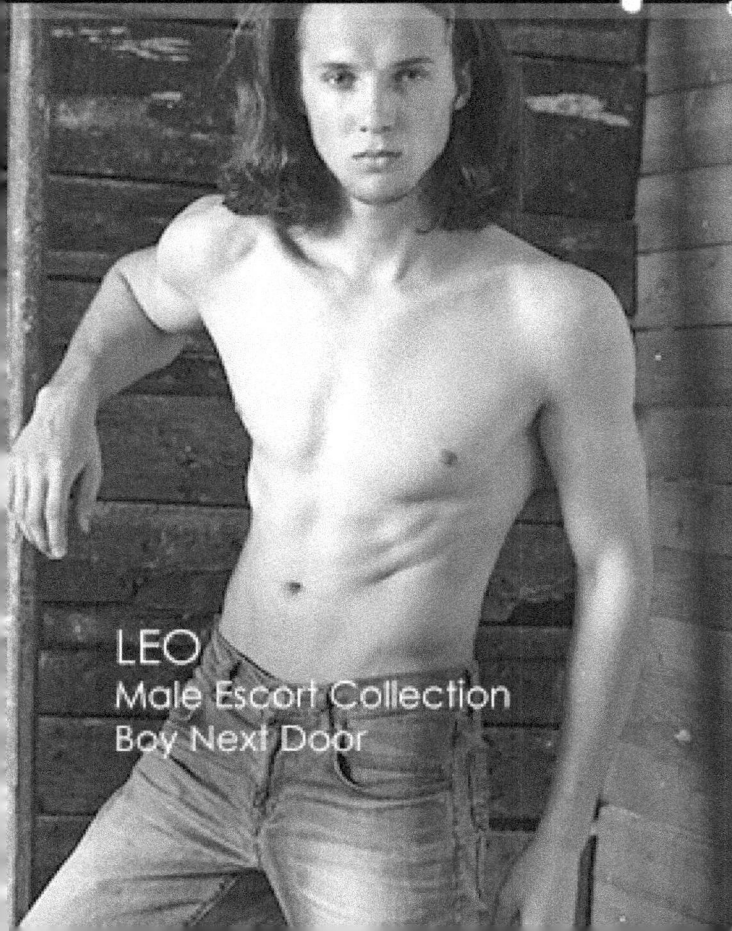

LEO
Male Escort Collection
Boy Next Door

NEIL
Play-Boy Collection
Boy Next Door

Madam Photo
A FREEBIRD PUBLISHERS COMPANY

JESSIE
Play-Girl Collection
White

Page Turning Books

EROTIC BOOKS

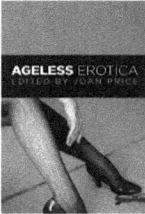

Ageless Erotica, by Joan Price
332 pages, $26.00 plus $4 S/H
Ground breaking, titillating, and libido charring, here is a collection of full sex stories that seniors can relate to. Some of the tales are tender and loving, while others are edgy and kinky.

Anything for You: Erotica for Kinky Couples, Ed. by Rachel Kramer Bussel
206 pages, $22.00 plus $4 S/H
Unravel a world of obsessive passion with these bold tales of sexual control and unbridled kink. Whether you are a BDSM aficionado or a novice newly discovering the joys of tying up your lover, this collection of great, uninhibited, adventurous sex stories has something for everyone.

Backstage, by Nikki Turner
248 pages, $20.00 plus $4 S/H
The Undisputed Queen of Hip-Hop Fiction presents five knock-out tales set in the fast-paced, high-stakes rap game, written by a hot lineup of authors with unmistakable swag and a gift for dropping sexy, thrilling stories.

Because You Are Mine, by Beth Kery
360 pages, $22.00 plus $4 S/H
From a private jet to an interlude in Paris, from a daring tryst in a public museum to the intimacy of a luxury hotel, Francesca and Ian come together whenever the need is aroused. As their relationship grows more intense, Francesca discovers something about Ian - and herself.

Best Lesbian Erotica 2008, by Tristan Taormino
254 pages, $23.00 plus $4 S/H
Best Lesbian Erotica 2008 journeys into the world of lesbian sex with uncommon, edgy stories that push lesbian lust and desire to new heights. Edited by bestselling author Tristan Taormino and selected and introduced by the dynamic Sister Spit performer Ali Liebegott, this latest edition of the best-selling lesbian erotica series in America is sensual, inventive, and breathtaking.

The Big Book of Bondage, Alison Tyler
332 pages, $21.00 plus $4 S/H
Surrender to your fantasies. Every submissive willingly does: bound or helpless, expecting the edctasy of her master's lash. Never mind the leaher-clothed or naked, she is stripped down to only the most basic physical and emotional need, completely exposed. The sensual stories that Aliston Tyler has assembeled in this collection delve into the dynamics of relationships filled with such unrestrained passion, revealing a world of beautiful contradictions that will thrill and inspire you.

Page Turning Books

The Big Book of Orgasms: 69 Sexy Stories, ED. by Rachel Kramer Bussel
354 pages, $22.00 plus $4 S/H
Sixty-nine top erotica writers serve up steamy scenarios, all focus on the Big O. The characters featured in these stories have fun exploring their desires and reaching new depths of pleasure with lovers who range from sweet to sweetly kinky.

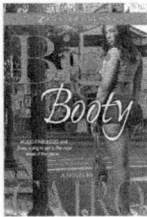

Big Booty, by Cairo
437 pages, $26.00 plus $4 S/H
Born in the projects and bred in the streets, Cassandra has been on her own since age 14. She learned how to make a way out of no way - from boosting clothes to credit card scams to sex. Unfortunately for her, seducing men out of their money came easily.

Blush, by Opal Carew
264 pages, $23.00 plus $4 S/H
Hanna Lane wishes she could unleash her wild side in the bedroom. When she meets J.M. - Kama Sutra and Trantic master. They embark on a sizzling path of discovery, exploring the ancient sensual arts and new techniques.

Bound by Lust, by Shanna Germain
242 pages, $16.00 plus $4 S/H
Imagine a partner who is just as naughty and kinky as you. A lover who wanders hardware stores with you in search on new toys,' a man who can wrangle both you and the dishes into submission, a woman who accompanies you to office parties and play parties. Bound by Lust is a romantic, couples-focused erotica with a BDSM slant. The couples range from newly blossoming relationships, long-time loves and reunited flames, bondage, spanking, domination, submission, power-play, pain and pleasure, or whatever your dirty mind can think of.

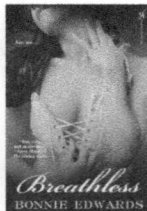

Breathless, by Bonnie Edwards
307 pages, $17.00 plus $4 S/H
Three novellas of ceaselessly steamy passion. In Breathless, a mysterious corset transports Blue to the year 1913 as a lush-bodied beauty. In "To Die For," Tawny turns to PI Stack Hamilton to uncover her luscious desires. And an artist needs inspiration in "Body by Gibson," she turns to her hard-bodied muse, carpenter Danny Glenn.

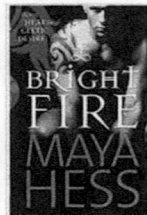

Bright Fire, by Maya Hess
239 pages, $14.00 plus $4 S/H
Thrown back two thousand years in time when her light aircraft crashes in an unusual storm, Jenna is revered as a "goddess from the shy" by the Celtic people in iron-age Britain.

Call Girl Confidential: An Escort's Secret Life as an Undercover Agent, by Rebecca Kade.
230 pages, $22.00 plus $4 S/H
You've heard of Anna Gristina, the "Soccer Mom Madam" who allegedly operated a multimillion dollar escort service with clients from the Forbes billionaires list to Capitol Hill. Now, discover the compelling, intimate story of the escort turned undercover agent who took the Soccer Mom Madam down.

By Mike Enemigo

The Care and Feeding of an Alpha Male, by Jessica Clare
329 pages, $17.00 plus $4 S/H
Beth Ann Williamson has finally had it with her fiancé of nine years. When she meets a die-hard survivalist, Colt Waggoner, and propositions him for a one-night stand, he knows he should turn it down. Because this alpha male might need more than one night in her bed to satisfy him.

Cheeky Spanking Stories, Ed. by Rachel Kramer Bussel
223 pages, $22.00 plus $4 S/H
From naughty and nice to fabulous and kinky, these stingingly good spanking stories will please aficionados as well as readers new to the ecstatic delights of the paddle, crop or hand. Adults only.

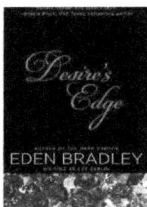

Desire's Edge, by Eden Bradley writing as E. Berlin
296 pages, $21.00 plus $4 S/H
As a lawyer, Kara Crawford knows how to keep a secret, especially after being spurned by an ex for revealing her sexual needs. She doesn't expect to find anyone who can fulfill her more extreme desires - until she meets sexual dominant Dante De Matteo.

Dirty Old Men: And Other Stories, by Omar Tyree
434 pages, $31.00 plus $4 S/H
Offers a daring collection of erotic tales about the undeniable attraction older men have for younger women.

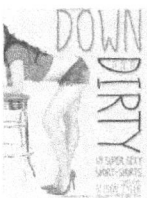

Down and Dirty: 69 Super Sexy Short-Shorts, Ed. by Alison Tyler
310 pages, $22.00 plus $4 S/H
The "Queen of the Quickie" offers a fresh collection of 69 scorching short stories that will leave you breathless with everything from sexy spankings and bondage to sex toys, voyeurism, exhibitionism, and more. Includes stories by Sage Vivant, N.T. Morley, Dante Davidson, and others.

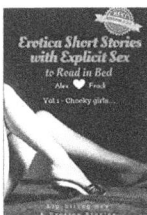

Erotica Short Stories with Explicit Sex to Read in Bed, Lip Biting Sex & Erotica Stories
264 pages, $16.00 plus $4 S/H
Erotica Short Stories with Explicit Sex to Read in Bed' is a tested series of erotica books for women, men and couples looking for lip-biting easy-to-read erotica with explicit sex! Think about it. Don't we all need nice, steamy and sexy short stories that can be read in bed, right before sleeping to finish our day with a little bit of privacy and fun?

Exit to Eden, by Anne Rice writing as A. Rampling
204 pages, $20.00 plus $4 S/H
Lisa, founder of an exclusive island resort, and a thrill-seeking photographer named Elliot find themselves involved in a journey to the limits of erotic pleasure and forbidden fantasy.

Page Turning Books

Exposing Casey, by Deanna Lee
247 pages, $29.00 plus $4 S/H
Casey Andrews loves the sex, but she wants to be loved as well. She thinks she may have found her answer in the Detective Shawn Tranner, but with someone bent on turning her dreams into nightmares, trusting the wrong person could be the last thing that Casey ever does.

Fanny Kill: Memoirs of a Woman of Pleasure, by John Cleveland
246 pages, $21.00 plus $4 S/H
Notorious story of a young woman's unconventional route to middle class respectability.

Fever, by Maya Banks
409 pages, $22.00 plus $4 S/H
Jace Crestwell and Ash McIntire have been best friends and successful business partners for years. They're powerful, they're imposing, they're irritably sexy, and Jace and Ash share everything - including their women. That is, until they meet Bethany.

Flying High: Sexy Stories from the Mile High Club, Ed. by Rachel Kramer Bussel.
187 pages, $22.00 plus $4 S/H
This gleeful guide to getting it on at 30,000 feet, complete with plenty ideas for membership into the Mile High Club, presents scintillating stories of one-flight-stand seductions by solo strangers, flirty flight attendants, cocky captains and passionate passengers.

Girl Crush, by R. Gay
226 pages, $19.00 plus $4 S/H
Every woman has a girl crush - that physical and emotional fascination with another provocative woman who inspires the thought, "What if?" Girl Crush answers that question with an inspiring range of erotic short stories about women acting on their desire and sometimes getting more than they bargained for.

Girls Who Score, by Ily Goyanes
192 pages, $21.00 plus $4 S/H
Girls who Score is a fresh entry into the field of lesbian erotica. In this one-of-a-kind anthology an all-star lineup of contributors present stories featuring hot female athletes who enjoy action on and off the sporting field. Girls Who Score is filled with complex, intriguing women who play hard and love harder.

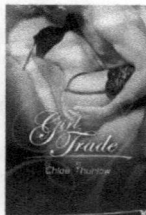

Girl Trade, by Chloe Thurlow
240 pages, $21.00 plus $4 S/H
Emily feels wicked, liberated, daring and bored. But her adventure begins in La Gomera, when a rugged beachcomber removes a leather thong from his neck and binds her hands behind her. Crossing oceans and continents in a nether world of smugglers, arms dealers, and pirates, she becomes the adored captive jewel of a tough inflexible man who makes a living in inhospitable landscapes. On hot afternoons on long days without number, she dedicates all of herself to him.

By Mike Enemigo

Hot City Nights, by Clara Darling
$21.00 plus $4 S/H
Two beautiful models suddenly find themselves rivals for the ultimate trophy: the title of Penthouse Pet of the Year.

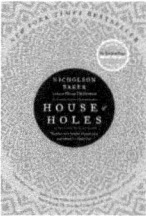

House of Holes: A Book of Raunch, by Nicholson Baker
262 pages, $23.00 plus $4 S/H
Shandee finds a gentle arm at a granite quarry. Ned drops down a hole in a golf course. Luna meets a man made of light bulbs at a tanning parlor. So begins Nicholson Baker's fuse-blowing, sex-positive escapade, set in a pleasure resort where the normal rules don't apply.

Hurts So Good, by Alison Taylor
232 pages, $21.00 plus $4 S/H
Intricately secured by ropes, locked in handcuffs or bound simple by a lover's command, the characters of Hurts So Good find themselves in the throes of pleasurable restraint in this new collection by prolific, award-winning editor Alison Tyler. Always playful and dangerously explicit, these arresting fantasies will grab you, tie you down and never let you go.

Insatiable: Porn - A Love Story, by Asa Akira
241 pages, $21.00 plus $4 S/H
In one of the most surprising books about sex in the 21st century, Akira offers a provocative memoir of her life and career as a porn star. Written with uncompromising honesty, her story is an electrifying, amusing, and sometimes disturbing look at a world still largely hidden from public view. Adults only.

Inside Linda Lovelace's Deep Throat: Degradation, Porno Chic, and the Rise of Feminism; by Darwin Porter
640 pages, $31.00 plus $4 S/H
She was a sex slave, the prisoner of a sadistic monster who rented her out for rape and became the party favor of Hollywood stars. In this overview of her life and times, new insights pour forth about the bizarre saga of the world's most famous porno star and the dark side of the American Dream.

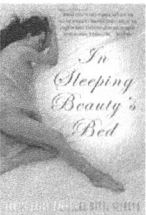

In Sleeping Beauty's Bed, by Mitzi Szereto
322 pages, $21.00 plus $4 S/H
Fairy tales are rich sources of sexual fantasy - sexy slippers, mattresses piled high, dominatrix witches, lustful princes, naked emperors... Seasoned erotica author Mitzi Szereto restores the sex in the 15 tales in this provocative book - and adds a few surprises of her own.

Instinctive, by Cathryn Fox
281 pages, $21.00 plus $4 S/H
Free-spirited Jaclyn is about to inherit a cosmetics empire, yet her scandalous personal history may ruin her chances for a clean corporate takeover. She moves to a gated community in New Hampshire, and soon learns that it's gated for a reason.

Page Turning Books

Irresistible, by Rachel Kramer Bussel
232 pages, $21.00 plus $4 S/H
Irresistible features loving couples who turn their deepest fantasies into reality -resulting in uninhibited, imaginative sex they can only enjoy together. Engage in a little sexting in A.M. Harnett's sizzling "Safe for Work" office tryst, and follow a kinky candidate for public office - and his lusty wife - in Alyssa Turner's intriguing "Hypocrites."

Jane Eyre Laid Bare, by Charlotte Bronte and E. Sinclair
322 pages, $21.00 plus $4 S/H
Presents a steamy, erotic re-imagining of Charlotte Bronte's tension-fueled tale, charting the smoldering sexual chemistry between the long-suffering governess and her brooding employer.

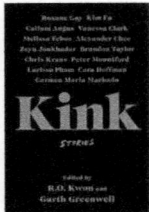

Kink, by Charlotte Bronte and E. Sinclair
322 pages, $21.00 plus $4 S/H
Kink is a dynamic anthology of literary fiction that opens an imaginative door into the world of desire. The stories within this collection portray love, desire, BDSM, and sexual kinks in all their glory with a bold new vision.

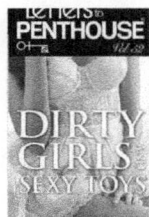

Letters to Penthouse, Vol. 52: Dirty Girls and Sexy Toys
336 pages, $21.00 plus $4 S/H
Toys aren't just for the playroom anymore. These signature Penthouse stories will confirm that almost anything can get you off with a little imagination. Whether it's solo or with a partner, a friend, or a even a Dom, our hot and helpful little gadgets will leave you with plenty of pleasure and good vibrations. So get ready for pocket rockets, whips and chains, and all types of rubber lovers. Strap on some fun, charge those batteries, and take a slippery trip to toy land that will leave you begging for more.

Letters to Penthouse, Vol. 53: Horney MILFS and Cougars on the Prowl
336 pages, $16.00 plus $4 S/H
Mrs. Robinson isn't the only cougar in town. There are plenty of yummy mummys and flirty forties just waiting to for a stud to make them feel young again. Penthouse readers know these sexy seductresses are experienced, insatiable and they don't play games...unless they're playing their boy-toys. Now, take an erotic journey to the suburbs where mature MILFs, wanton wives next door, and wicked widows are stalking their young prey.

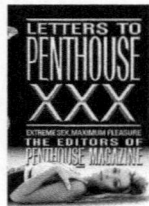

Letters to Penthouse XXX: Extreme Sex Maximum Pleasure
352 pages, $21.00 plus $4 S/H
Welcome to a milestone in the Penthouse revolution. And "XXX" marks the spot. The thirtieth volume of this bestselling series features special letters handpicked for their extremely sensual, provocative power. From wedding halls to frat houses, campgrounds to rock bars, truck stops to strip clubs, you can share in these ultimate escapades. There's nothing more hard-core than XXX!

Letters to Penthouse XXXXVI: Dirty Dares and Red Hot Hookups
304 pages, $21.00 plus $4 S/H
Imagine a world with no limits, one in which your wildest fantasies can, and do, come true. That's exactly what the readers of Penthouse have done in this collection of pulse-quickening letters. From sensual daydreams about hot coworkers to lusty fantasies of swashbuckling lotharios to couples' racy role-playing, Penthouse readers prove that there is no end to their erotic imagination.

By Mike Enemigo

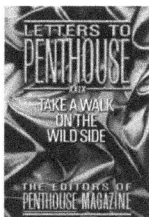

Letters to Penthouse XXIX: Take a Walk on the Wild Side
293 pages, $21.00 plus $4 S/H
Scintillating collection of short essays where men and women confess their kinkiest escapades. Adults only.

Letters to Penthouse XXXIV: Sinful Sirens and their Dirty Little Secrets
320 pages, $21.00 plus $4 S/H
Leave your inhibitions at the door and plunge right into these tales -sizzling with delight, each one steamier than the last. Adults only.

Lie to Me, by Tori St. Claire
337 pages, $16.00 plus $4 S/H
After helping to break up a Russian human trafficking ring, Alexi Nikanova's newest assignment is to rescue one of the stolen women and return her to her father. When he discovers his target is Sasha Zablosky, a woman who has haunted him since a tryst in Moscow, passions long dormant are reignited - even as a shadowy menace looms.

Lustfully Ever After, by Kristina Wright
232 pages, $21.00 plus $4 S/H
Even grown-ups need bedtime stories, and this delightful collection of fairy tales will lead you down a magical path into forbidden romance and erotic love. In Michelle Augello-Page's naughty \"Wolf Moon," Little Red Riding Hood herself is the big, bad wolf, while Kristina Lloyd reimagines "The Twelve Dancing Princesses" with a scorching hot threesome in "The Last Dance."

Maid to Order, by Penny Birch
252 pages, $21.00 plus $4 S/H
Penny's niece, Jemima is in disgrace and has been sent away to work in a hotel for the summer by her scheming step-mother, a woman who delights in bare bottom spankings. Not only is the hotel owner the notorious Morris Rathwell, organizer of the kinkiest parties in the country.

The Mammoth Book of Erotica by Maxim Jakubowski
624 Pages. $21.00 plus $4 S/H
A newly revised and updated edition of the bestselling collection of contemporary erotic fiction, this anthology of erotic short stories has been revised and expanded with new sensual tales especially commissioned for the volume.

Maneater, by M.B. Morrison and Noire
274 pages, $21.00 plus $4 S/H
Novellas. Mary B. Morrison pairs with the "Queen of Urban Erotica," Noire, to deliver two tantalizing stories about sex, revenge - and getting what you deserve. Includes Character of a Man and Sugar-Honey-Ice-Tee.

Page Turning Books

Monsieur, by Emma Becker
372 pages, $19.00 plus $4 S/H
An all-consuming affair between a young student and her mysterious older lover begins with their initial online encounter. Through a shared appreciation of erotic literature, to the shocking break-up of their brief relationship, Becker mines the depth to which love and lust can drive us.

On these Silken Sheets, by Sabrina Darby
387 pages, $21.00 plus $4 S/H
Hadrian House: it is Regency London's most exclusive after-hours club, catering to the erotic fantasies of randy lords and inquisitive ladies, each discreetly masked to guard every delicious indiscretion.

Peep Show, by Rachel Kramer Bussel
224 pages, $20.00 plus $4 S/H
Whether you love to watch a lover undress in person, relish peeking at the neighbors through a crack in their blinds, love to visit a strip club for a steamy show, or adore reversing the equation by taking center stage, Peep Show packs an erotic punch for voyeurs - and exhibitionists - of any stripe. This book corrals several unique stories, each of which explores a different facet of these desires, ensuring that any reader will be titillated.

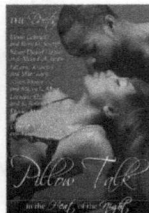

Pillow Talk in The Heat of the Night, by Elissa Gabrielle
368 pages, $29.00 plus $4 S/H
Through a smoldering written collaboration of lust, love and the pursuit of great sex, these authors take you on sizzling and sultry journeys of mouth-watering and titillating stories guaranteed to satisfy every fantasy or desire; while delivering a much deserved happy ending. Adults only.

Pleasure's Edge, by Eden Bradley writing as E. Berlin
294 pages, $21.00 plus $4 S/H
For beautiful novelist Dylan Ivory, being in control is everything. While researching a book on sexual extremes, Dylan interviews Alec Walker and long to tastes the temptation he offers. But he's a self-proclaimed dominate and she refuses to surrender control.

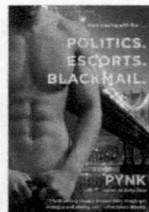

Politics, Escorts, Blackmail; by Pynk.
326 pages, $21.00 plus $4 S/H
The CEO of Lip Service, NYC's most exclusive escort company, Money knows how to keep her talented stable in line and give the city's top cop all the punishment he craves. In this world of high stakes and hot desire, nothing is forbidden, except exposing Lip Service's most dangerous secrets. Adults only.

Pure Sex, by Lucinda Betts et al.
265 pages, $19.00 plus $4 S/H
Novellas, it's not what you want it's what you need. It's what you crave -three hot stories that are 100 percent pure sex: The Bet by Lucinda Betts; Slow Hand by Bonnie Edwards; and The Crib by Sasha White.

By Mike Enemigo

Saddled Up, by Penny Birch
208 pages, $31.00 plus $4 S/H
Amber Oakley is back. Determined as ever to avoid getting her bottom smacked but her own deep needs and the awkward circumstances she finds herself in trying to solve her financial difficulties mean otherwise. Offering riding tuition to girls from wealthy families seems like a good idea, but Portia and Ophelia Crowthorne-Jones prove to have a few ideas of their own, and are soon indulging both their lesbian desires and their cruel sense of humor at Amber's expanse.

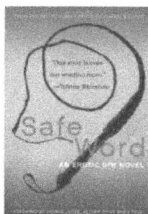

Safe Word, by Molly Weatherfield
250 pages, $21.00 plus $4 S/H
The sequel to Carrie's Story. Leaving her lover and master behind, Carrie's got a tougher guy in charge now. Groomed, collared, and harnessed to his exact specifications, Carrie finds herself and a fantasy netherworld of lovely "ponies," where she learns to play and win some dangerous erotic games.

The Secret Life of Girls, Chloe Thurlow
208 pages, $29.00 plus $4 S/H
After the gardner spanks her bottom and a nun at finishing school seduces her in the catacombs, Bella realizes that sex was what she was born for. She adores wearing dildos and deflowering virgins as much as she adores indulging roguish Chris with his addiction to bondage. Then her world tumbles when she learns her beloved Ickham Manor doesn't belong to her, but her wicked stepfather.

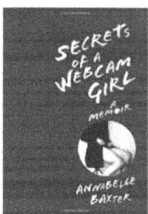

Secrets of a Webcam Girl, by Annabelle T. Baxter
260 pages, $22.00 plus $4 S/H
This is the true story of a woman's transition from business suit to birthday suit as a way to solve mounting financial problems. Told with candor and wit, this behind the scenes memoir reveals her patrons' fetishes, infidelities, and perversities while offering stunning revelations. Adults only.

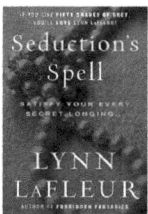

Seduction's Spell, by Lynn LaFleur
310 pages, $20.00 plus $4 S/H
In North Texas sits a charming antebellum mansion, an intimate resort that exists for one purpose alone: to bring couples together by fulfilling their every secret longing and satisfying their most sensuous needs.

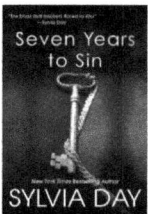

Seven Years to Sin, by Sylvia Day
341 pages, $21.00 plus $4 S/H
A young man forced to sell his body for money. A young lady who watched him do it. Two tormented souls brought together years later to assuage the hunger of a desperate, irresistible attraction.

Sexual Exploits of a Nympho, by Richard Jeanty
215 pages, $21.00 plus $4 S/H
Tina develops an insatiable sexual appetite very early in life. She only loves her boyfriend, Darren, but he's too far away in college to satisfy her sexual needs. Tina decided to get buck wild away in college and she sleeps with more than enough of her share of men. Will her sexual tryst jeopardize the lives of the men in her life?

Page Turning Books

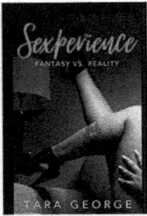

Sexperience, by Tara George
250 pages, $26.00 plus $4 S/H
Work by day, temptress by night, Tara have it all- wealth, power and a world full of possibilities. Yet dealing with her troubled past, she ventures into the world taking on a promiscuous life style. From tall dark and handsome to short and sweet. It is hard to keep up with all the guys she meets. We are not one for spoilers, but the steaminess of this book will have you ready to pull out your handcuffs, whips, tassels and more.

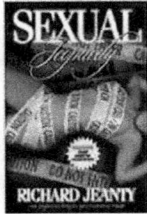

Sexual Jeopardy, by Richard Jeanty
250 pages, $21.00 plus $4 S/H
Ronald Murphy was a player all his life until he and his best friend, Myles, met the women of their dreams during a brief vacation in South Beach, Florida. Shauna was every man's dream physically and intellectually, but she wasn't always careful and selective when it came to men. The most important requirement to her was the size of their wallet.

Secret Lives, by Thea Devine
304 pages, $16 plus $4 S/H
When her twin sister disappears, Justine Durant masqerades as Jillian in order to search for clues. Soon she plunges into a world of paid carnal extravagance, unleashing a side of herself she never knew existed.

She's on Top, by Susan Lyons
341 pages, $26.00 plus $4 S/H
They call themselves the Awesome Foursome - four girlfriends who share everything, except their men. They have found the ultimate in lust and love and now it's Rina's turn.

Show and Tell, by Nioba Bryant
246 pages, $29.00 plus $4 S/H
A sizzling, provocative follow-up to Live and Learn, exploring the bonds among four friends (Alize, Moet, "Dom" Peringnon, and Cristal) who are about to discover that getting your desires met can sometimes cost you everything.

Sinful Harvest, by Anitra Lynn McLeod
298 pages, $20.00 plus $4 S/H
In the erotically charged world of the Harvesters, taking a woman's virginity is a man's greatest responsibility. Kerrick performs his duties like a champion, but when his leaders decide to turn the tables, Kerrick finds himself the sexual servant of his destined mate, and fiery beauty Ariss.

Slippery When Wet, by Cairo
287 pages $22.00 plus $4 S/H
Offers up five salacious stories, filled to the brim with sizzling steamy erotica for anyone who enjoys, fantasizes about, or simply craves girl-girl sex. Contributions by Ava Wilson, Miasha Simmons, Laila Reynolds, and Reggie Sanders. Adults only.

Smooth, by Rachel Kramer Bussel
204 pages, $23.00 plus $4 S/H
The caress of skin against skin, the warmth of another's touch, relishing the sight that few others get to see - these are the reasons that disrobing before sex can be so gratifying. Read along as women get tattooed, become "the sushi girl" at a restaurant, strip on the subway, go commando, host tea parties, enjoy sloshing and much more.

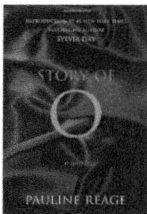

Story of O
240 pages, $20.00 plus $4 S/H
How far will a woman go to express her love? In this exquisite novel of passion and desire, the answer emerges through a daring exploration of the deepest bonds of sensual domination. "O" is a beautiful Parisian fashion photographer, determined to understand and prove her consuming devotion to her lover, René, through complete submission to his every whim, his every desire. It is a journey of forbidden, dangerous choices that sweeps her through the secret gardens of the sexual underground.

Stripped, by Tori St. Claire
402 pages, $24.00 plus $4 S/H
As a member of the CIA's elite Black Opals, Natalya Trubachev must live a lie, working undercover as the lover of Dimitri, a Russian mob boss. His business is trafficking vulnerable Las Vegas strippers overseas for twisted sex games.

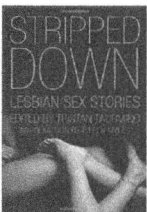

Stripped Down, by Tristan Taormino
328 pages, $16.00 plus $4 S/H
Where else but a Tristan Taormino erotica collection can you find a femme vigilante, a virgin baby butch, and a snake charmer jostling for your attention? The salacious stories in Stripped Down draw you in like honeyed voices from an upstairs room. In Peggy Munson's "Into the Baptismal," two farm girls decide to test their virginity pledges one rainy summer night.

Sunstone Vol.1, by Stjepan Sejic
128 pages, $21.00 plus $4 S/H
Two women deal with modern themes of sex, relationships, and fetishism in this erotic romantic comedy. So beware all who enter, because, to quote a few hundred thousand readers on DeviantArt: "I'm not into BDSM...but this story...I get it."

Sunstone Vol.2, by Stjepan Sejic
128 pages, $21.00 plus $4 S/H
The hotly-anticipated second volume of the BDSM romance graphic novel that (consensualy) took the world by storm! Originally a webcomic sensation, Sunstone is an erotic romantic comedy about fetishism, sexuality and relationships.

Sunstone Vol.3, by Stjepan Sejic
128 pages, $21.00 plus $4 S/H
Ally and Lisa are happy, well-adjusted young women, but they're both a little lonely. Ally loves the creativity of being a "domme" in her sex life, but hasn't found the right person to share it with. And Lisa... well, Lisa loves to be tied up! When they find each other online, they know they have to meet. But bondage is all about trust, and even after they've explored every facet of their sexuality together, Ally and Lisa will find the ultimate test of this trust lies in three simple words.

Sunstone Vol.4, by Stjepan Sejic
160 pages, $21.00 plus $4 S/H
Stjepan Sejic continues the critically acclaimed Sunstone series with Volume 4. A classy, sexy, fun, and emotional look at two women and the alternative lifestyle they live. It's all fun and games until someone falls in love! But the fun and games carry on!

Sunstone Vol.5, by Stjepan Sejic
264 pages, $21.00 plus $4 S/H
One honest smile at a time. Lisa thought this, for a moment at least. It was a hopeful thought... but it was wishful thinking. it takes more than smiles. It takes words, courage, and actions. This is where they finish the first arc, but they'll be back. Like doms, writers too must know when to be cruel, and when to show mercy!

Sunstone Vol.6, by Stjepan Sejic
264 pages, $21.00 plus $4 S/H
How can you teach a broken heart to trust again? How can you embrace each other with hands clinging to your past? Why do you always need to pee after I tie you up?
Anne and Alan have more than a few questions to answer as we expand on the story of Sunstone with this new story

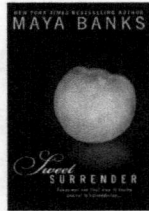

Sweet Surrender, by Myra Banks
344 pages, $16.00 plus $4 S/H
Under Faith Malone's deceptively soft exterior lies a woman who knows exactly what she wants: a strong man who'll take without asking, because she's willing to give him everything. That's where Dallas cop Gray Montgomery comes in.

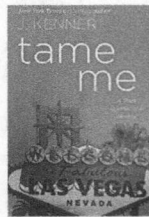

Tame Me, by J.Kenner
129 pages, $15.00 plus $4 S/H
Aspiring actress Jamie Archer is on the run. From herself. From her wild child ways. From the screwed up life that she left behind in Los Angeles. And, most of all, from Ryan Hunter—the first man who has the potential to break through her defenses to see the dark fears and secrets she hides.Stark International Security Chief Ryan Hunter knows only one thing for sure—he wants Jamie. Wants to hold her, make love to her, possess her, and claim her. Wants to do whatever it takes to make her his.But after one night of bliss, Jamie bolts. And now it's up to Ryan to not only bring her back, but to convince her that she's running away from the best thing that ever happened to her--him.

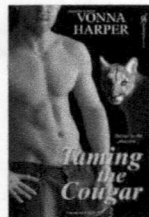

Taming the Cougar, by Vonna Harper
281 pages, $18.00 plus $4 S/H
Deep in the canyons of Arizona, animal psychic Kai Tallon senses something is watching her. This is the land of the Tocho - half man/half cougars borne of the Navajo, said to possess unearthly masculine prowess. Could they be real? In one wild night of pleasure, she will discover the truth.

Testimony, by Kenneth Jackson
241 pages, $16.00 plush $4 S/H
A novel of sizzling short stories filled with realistic, fascinating imaginative dramas, inappropriate sexual behaviors and spontaneous thought's and act's. A beautiful and exciting read, written for your enjoyment by the creative mind of Kenneth Jackson.

By Mike Enemigo

Testimony: The Sequel, by Kenneth Jackson
250 pages, $16.00 plus $4 S/H
Testimony The Sequel A novel of sizzling short stories filled with realistic, fascinating imaginative dramas, inappropriate sexual behaviors and spontaneous thought's and act's. A beautiful and exciting read, written for your enjoyment by the creative mind of Kenneth Jackson.

Three, by Noelle Mack
277 pages, $16.00 plus $4 S/H
Lady Fiona Gilberte, a sensual, enigmatic beauty, is presently without a husband, but never without a lover. With a vast wealth, an elegant Mayfair mansion, and a staff of servants, Lady Fiona does as she pleases. Then she meets Edward Delamar, the most virile lover she has ever known.

Three in a Bed, by Monica Belle
224 pages, $18.00 plus $4 S/H
Small, pretty, pleasant, and a bit of a geek, Paige is the perfect employee for Araminta, the feisty owner of the Lifelong Dating Agency. She's certainly not the sort of person to stand up to her domineering boss and even less likely to go out on dates with sexually demanding strangers until one day she finds herself in a position where she has very little choice but to acquiesce in the intimate peculiar requests of Lifelong Agency's clients; leading to Mrs. Anderson to show her who's boss.

Threesome, by Miranda Forbes
208 pages, $31.00 plus $4 S/H
Threesome - When One Lover Is Not Enough is a collection of twenty varied stories with ménage a' trois themes. All combinations of couplings are explored allowing the reader to indulge in a fiction feast of ménage a' trois naughtiness.

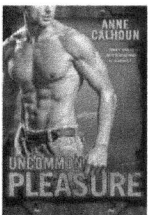

Uncommon Pleasure, by Anne Calhoun
294 pages, $15.00 plus $4 S/H
Novellas. The tale of two women, each daring to challenge the boundaries of the toughest men. In these edgy, heated encounters, the greatest living thing each woman will risk is her heart. Contains Over the Edge and All on the Line.

Venus and Serena Williams: Sexy Photo Booklet, by Marlow Martin
78 pages, $26.00 plus $4 S/H
Venus and Serena sexy photos like no one has ever seen them before!

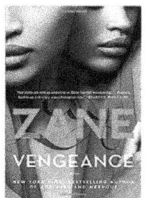

Vengeance: A Novel, by Zane
288 pages, $18.00 plus $4 S/H
From New York Times bestselling author Zane comes a thrilling erotic novel, set in the same world of Addicted and Nervous, featuring a beautiful but emotionally damaged pop star hell-bent on vengeance against the people responsible for her traumatic past.

Page Turning Books

Vox, by Nicholson Baker
176 pages, $21.00 plus $4 S/H
Vox is a novel that remaps the territory of sex—sex solitary and telephonic, lyrical and profane, comfortable and dangerous. It is an erotic classic that places Nicholson Baker firmly in the first rank of major American writers.

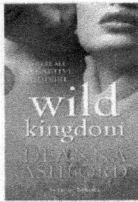

Wild Kingdom, by Deanna Ashford
260 pages, $26.00 plus $4 S/H
Salacious excesses abound as war rages in the mythical kingdom of Kabra. When Baroness Crissana presents Rainna as a plaything to her warlord half-brother, prince Tarn is forced to join his old enemy Sarin, whose capacity for perverse delights known no bounds, to get her back.

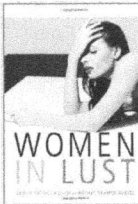

Women in Lust, by Rachel Kramer Bussel
224 pages, $16.00 plus $4 S/H
Whether watching a lover playing guitar, using a webcam, going out for a smoke or simply embracing a chance encounter, these women seize the opportunities presented to them, and savor the lovers who teach them about themselves and help them open up to new sensual possibilities. These women embrace lust even when it makes them do things they might consider reckless.

Working It, by Jordan Monroe
254 pages, $18.00 plus $4 S/H
Everybody's working it, grinding away at the 9 to 5, when what we really want to do is take a hot tumble on the boss' desk. Let this sexy collection whisk you away from the daily grind of the workaday world and into sixteen stories that explore sex where you least expect it.

XII Angels, by Stephen Lehman
150 pages, $41.00 plus $4 S/H
Smokin' hot sexy women color photo book with gloss pages. All non-nude photos which push all the boundaries. XII Angels includes provocative photos of women in all poses imaginable.

All books are available for purchase through Freebird Publishers by mail:
Freebird Publishers
221 Pearl St., Ste. 541
North Dighton, MA 02764
or online at FreebirdPublishers.com

By Mike Enemigo

SECRETS
WOMEN
WISHED
YOU KNEW

A Caring Guy is a Hot Guy

What do women want? For those who have ever pondered this question, here are 19 relationship secrets. They're based on the study of healthy, happy couples and our changing gender roles. Secret No. 1: Women appreciate a guy with a sensitive side, especially when they're upset. Put your arm around them and hand them a tissue. Nurturing is a powerful way to connect.

Chivalry Still Has a Place

When it comes to romance, many women do like men to take a traditional masculine role. This is especially true in the wooing stage of a relationship, according to psychologist Diana Kirschner, PhD, who's written several books about love. They are perfectly capable of pulling out their own chair or opening a door, but if you see them hesitate, they might just be waiting for you to be the gentleman.

Dress to Impress

Styles come and go, but men's attention to their grooming and clothing should be long lasting. It's important to women from the first flirtation through the honeymoon and beyond. "You've got to figure out if there's a certain look that she likes," says Kirschner. "If she likes a guy in tight jeans, you wear tight jeans."

Guy Wears Red, Guy Gets Girl

OK, this tip doesn't come from women, but from clever testing by psychologists of women's subconscious preferences. One intriguing study found that the color red made men seem more powerful, attractive, and sexually desirable to women. There's a caveat, though. Red doesn't make guys appear nicer or kinder. That part is up to you.

Don't Hide Your Flaws

Nothing captures a woman's heart quite like a good man who wants to be a better man, according to love guru Kirschner. "Women love personal growth, they love a man who is thoughtful and sensitive." They like it when their men recognize a flaw -- a short temper, for example, or a regularly sullen mood after work -- and love it when they make an effort to address it.

Don't Try To Fix Their World

When something's bothering them, they want your ear, not your advice. "Men feel the need to fix things because they are solution-oriented," says Kirschner. "But to a woman, really listening is a wonderful, wonderful thing that deepens the relationship."

Women Like The Slow Lane

Guys often want to take the quickest path to sex. But many women prefer the scenic route. "Women want sex but they get to it in a different way," says psychologist Kirschner, who has helped hundreds of couples achieve a more rewarding relationship. "They want to feel connected and understood, they want to be romanced." That means time and talking and touching -- in other words, foreplay.

Learn What They Want In Bed

Women do like to talk to about what's going on in the sack, and they want to please their man -- and a tactful approach is often best. Ask them what they like. Be sure to ask for what you want in a positive and validating way. Kirschner advises saying something along the lines of, "I would really love if you [fill in the blanks]."

Mirroring Is A Barometer of Love

Remember the saying "imitation is the highest form of flattery"? A woman often conveys how they feel about you by mirroring your moods and moves. They may order a meal that pairs with yours, wear your favorite color, or smile or cross their arms when you do. Mimicking is their way of putting you at ease and letting you know they are charmed.

Look Your Partner In the Eye

You may feel more comfortable sitting side by side, but women prefer face time – and we don't mean the latest mobile video chat technology. Kirschner says that women prefer their men to make eye contact with them as they're talking. And looking her in the eye during sex will deepen the relationship outside the bedroom.

Reprinted from WebMD Men's Health

Sex Tapes

PROD.NO.
SCENE   TAKE   SOUND
DIRECTOR
CAMERAMAN
DATE
PRODUCED   EXT.   INT.

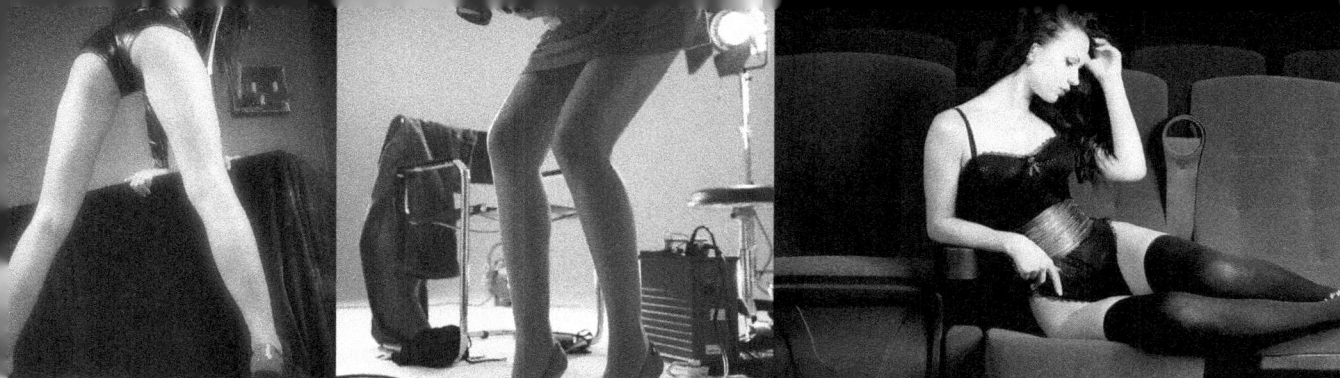

SEX TAPES

Wrapped just right for you.

Nubian Princess, Chanail, now offers the following sex tapes for your listening pleasure.

1. Frankie LaRue, Katrina, Caramel and Monique. Approx. 45 minutes of hot bump and grind action. $22.00

2. Monique, Ice, Skyy, Mercury and Ayanna Angel. Approx. 45 minutes of hot bump and grind action. $22.00

3. Ayana Angel, Promise, Carmen Jones, Lil Assinie and Coco Girl. Approx. 45 minutes of hot bump and grind action. $22.00

4. Japan, Chloe Black, Shanea, Coco Princess, Katy, Victoria Summer, and Carlina. Approx. 45 minutes. Hot bump and grind action. $22.00

5. Bianca, Delmar, Roxy, Cinnamen, Envy, Lisa, Vanessa and Nina. Approx. 45 minutes of hot bump and grind action. $22.00

6. Dominique Simone, Lola Lane, Monique, Chyna and Mya, Diana DeVoe, Dede Lopez, Sunshine, Nikki Lane and Insaciable. Approx 45 minutes of hot bump and grind action. $22.00

7. Crystal Knight, Bettina, Imani Rose, Ayana Angel and Jennifer Steele. Approx. 45 minutes of hot bump and grind action. $22.00

8. Gabryelly Dumont (T/S), Sandy Lopes (T/S), Rafinha Angel (T/S), Pamela Gaucha (T/S), Neffetti (T/S), and Noguira (T/S). $22.00

9. Teddi Bear, Cherokee D'Ass, Mercedes Ashley, Lilmomma, Hazel, Ayana Angel, Ebony Barbie, and Juicy. Approx. 45 minutes of hot bump and grind action. $22.00

10. Asian and Latin ladies Yume Kawaii, Kimmi Kanni, Tammy Lee, Kami, Sami Moon, Gin Seng, Kat, Ice LaFox and Jasmine. Hot bump and grind action. $22.00

11. Latin and Asian ladies Savita Rolle, Megan Martinez, Jasmine, Ange Venus and Kaila Mai. Hot bump and grind action. $22.00

12. Hear me (porn star Chanail) talk. I will send you a 15-minute cassette of me moaning, groaning and cumming for just $15.00.

13. Send me your name, and I will make a dirty sex tape just for you. For 20 minutes you will hear me moan, groan and cum while I say your name. Just $40.00

To order any of the above tapes, send institutional check or money order to:
Nubian Princess Entertainment; PO Box 37; Timmonsville, S.C. 29161

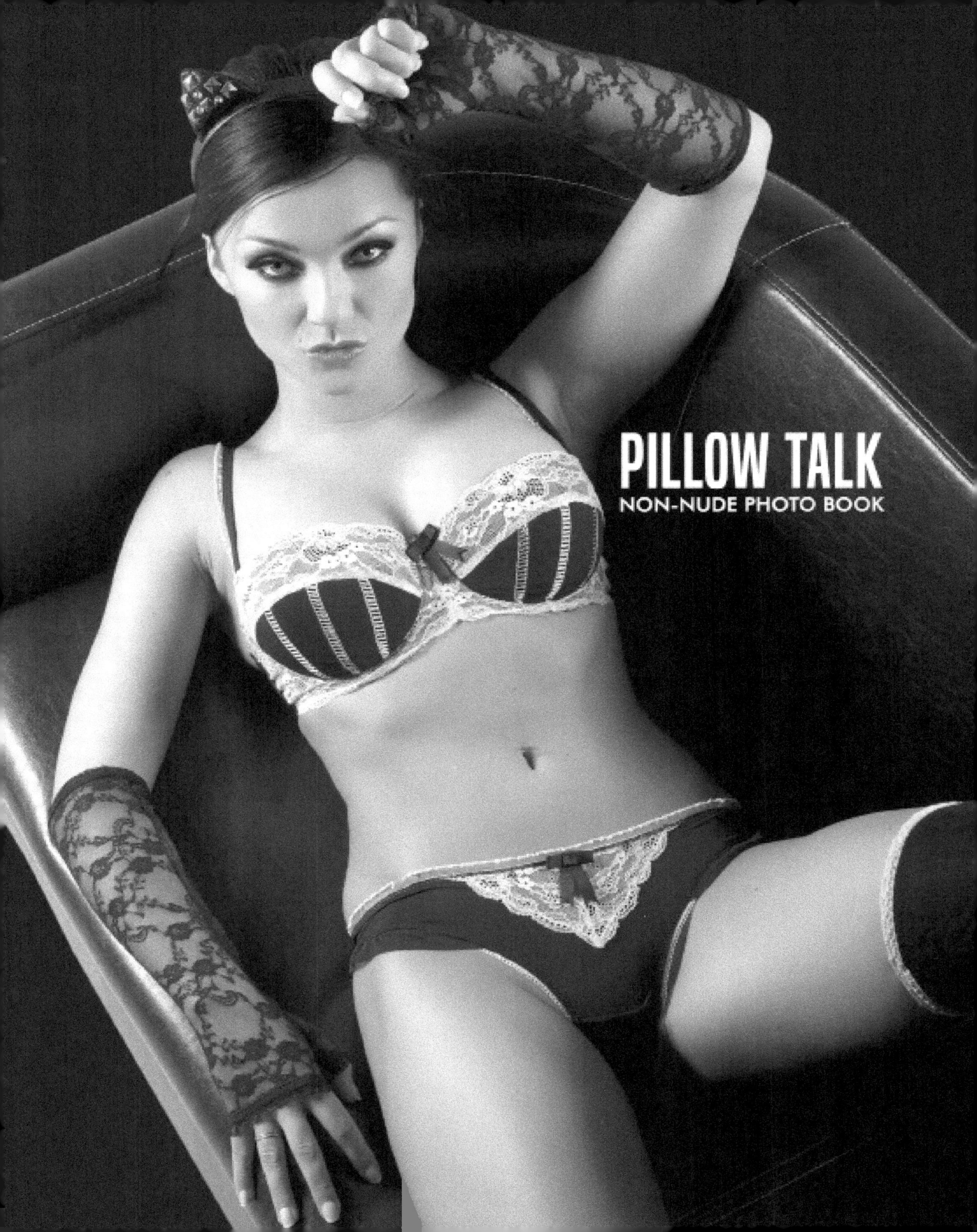
PILLOW TALK
NON-NUDE PHOTO BOOK

PILLOW TALK
NON-NUDE PHOTO BOOK

PILLOW TALK

NON-NUDE PHOTO BOOK

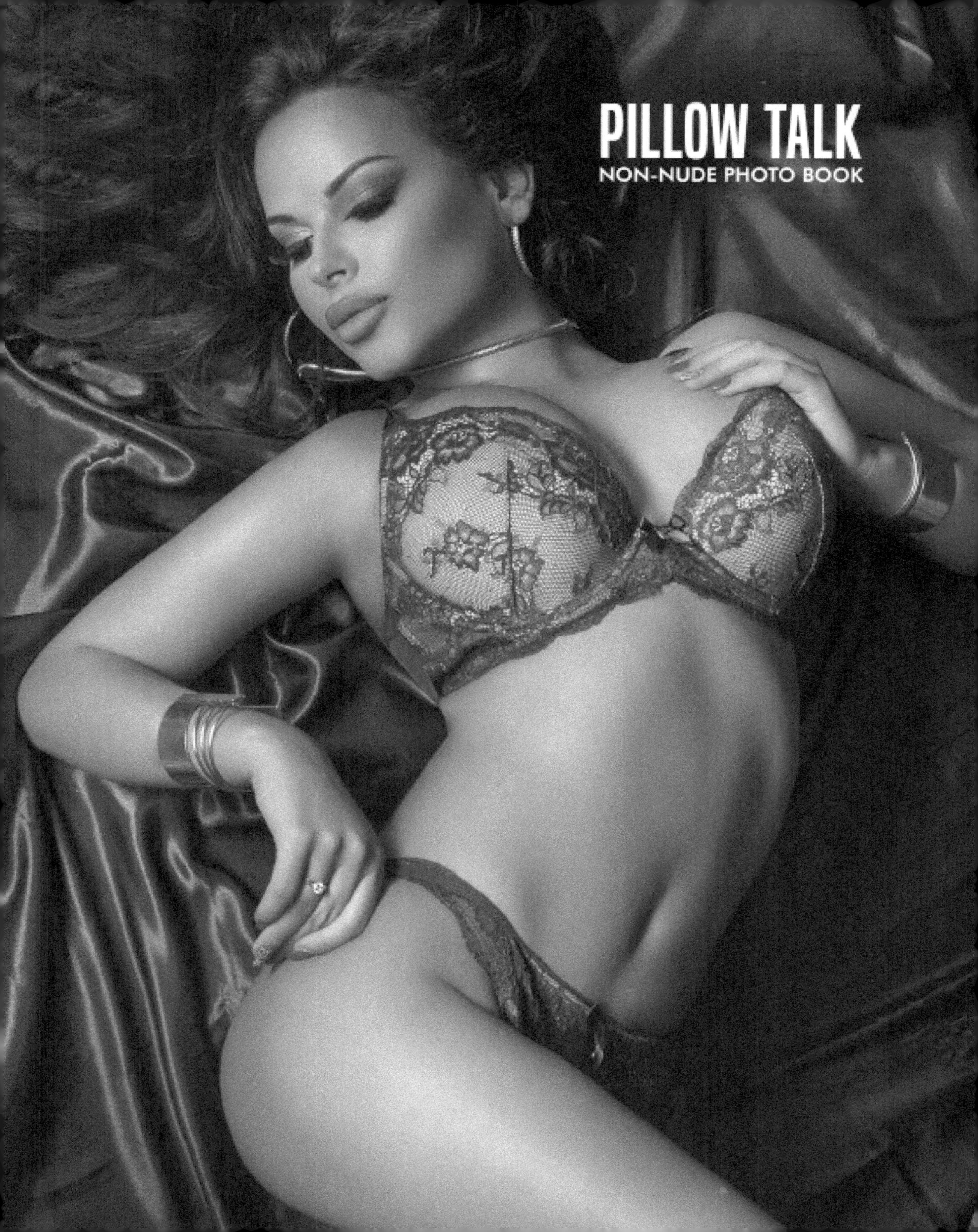
PILLOW TALK
NON-NUDE PHOTO BOOK

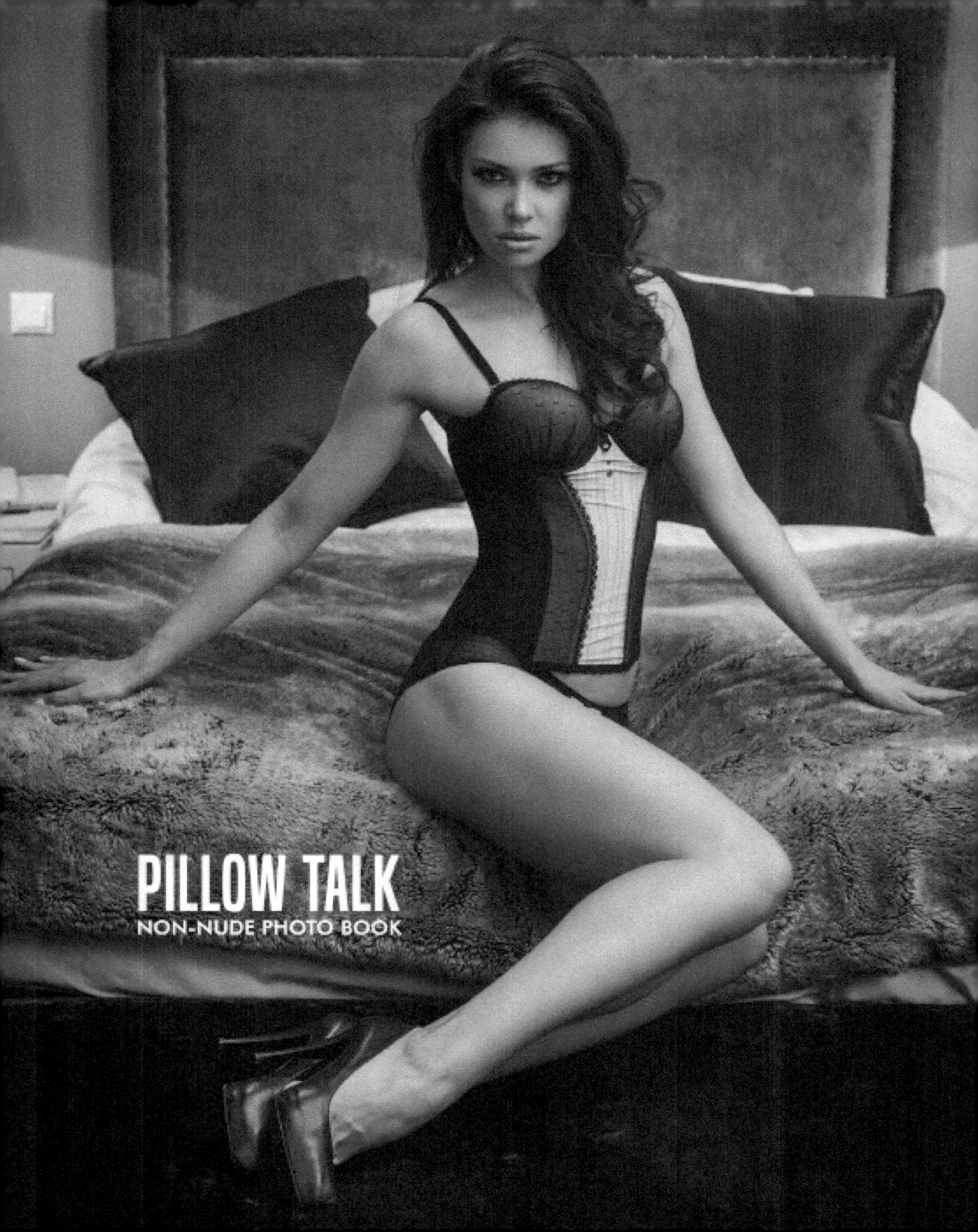

PILLOW TALK

NON-NUDE PHOTO BOOK

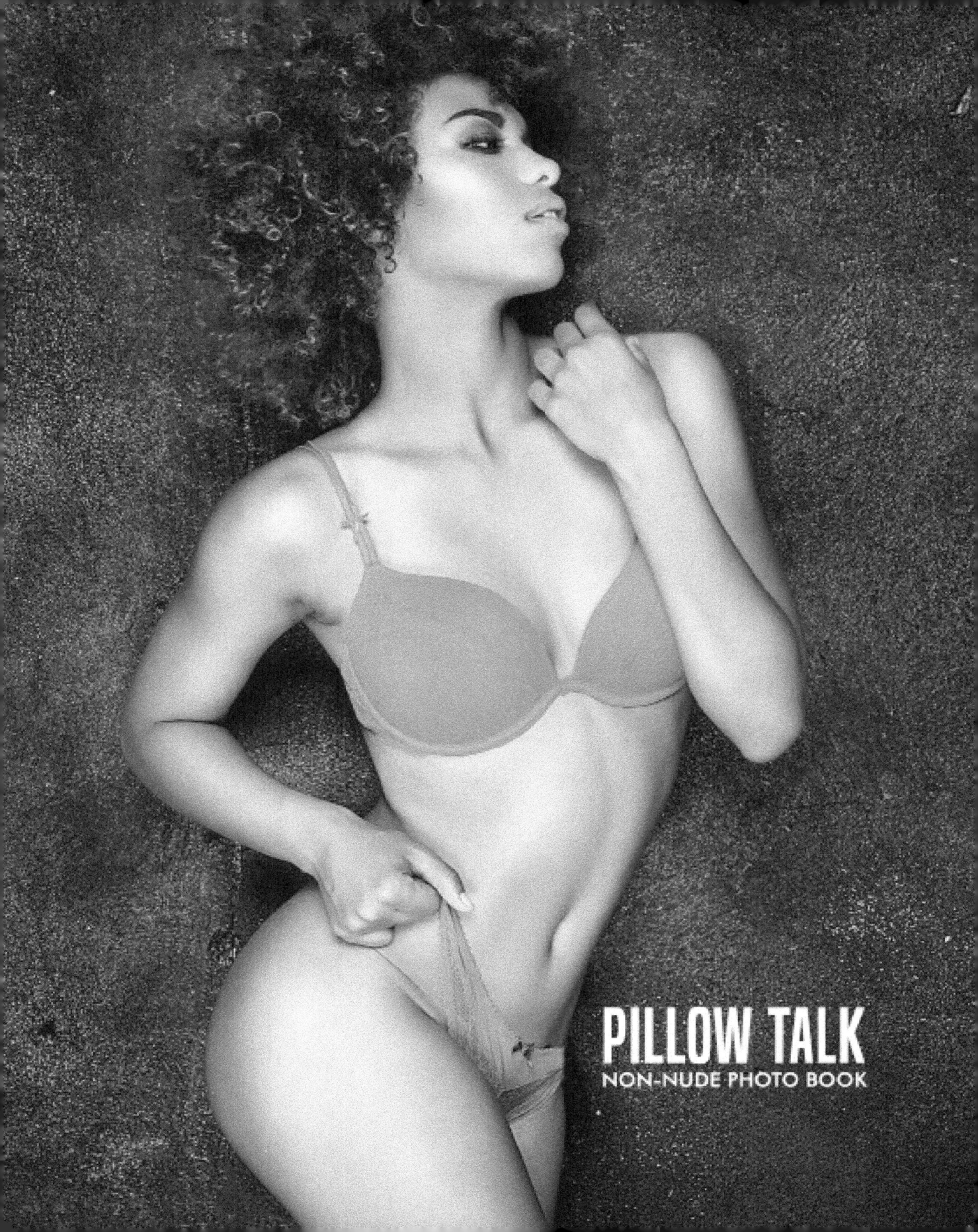

PILLOW TALK
NON-NUDE PHOTO BOOK

PILLOW TALK

NON-NUDE PHOTO BOOK

Kitty Kat: Adult Entertainment Non Nude Resource Book

Strip Clubs

4Play
2238 Cotner Ave.

Los Angeles CA, 90064

All Gentlemen know, when in L.A., 4PLAY comes first. Conveniently located in L.A.'s prestigious westside, where the 10 and 405 freeways meet near Beverly Hills and Santa Monica. 4Play is able to present beautiful ladies 7 days a week because of their reputation, connections within Hollywood, the modeling industry, and other private and privileged resources.

On any given night listen to our DJ's playing the latest and most erotic songs for our Full Nude stage shows. While you watch the show you might look around and catch a glimpse of a celebrated musician, actor, sports star, or business magnate rubbing elbows with our other VIP guests. All while enjoying the company and attention of one of our variety of ladies: Playmates, models, weather girls, tv hostesses, and good old fashioned girls next door.

4PLAY is the perfect venue for large bachelor, birthday, or retirement parties, and VIP Bottle Service is at the ready should you wish to celebrate in high style. They also have private themed rooms for a secluded lap dance or intimate rendezvous with the ladies of your choosing. Simply contact one of our Managers with your needs and they will tailor all our resources to your situation. Pampering and luxury are NOT an option, but rather a standard amenity with every visit.

2001 Odyssey
2309 N Dale Mabry Hwy.
Tampa, FL 33607

The best full nude strip club in Tampa for 14 years. Boasting their "out of this world" entertainers of all nationalities, heights, shapes and personalities with a actual spaceship VIP room located on the clubs rooftop. Private lapdance rooms, private champagne rooms

Strip Clubs

Acropolis Steakhouse

33-02 Queens Blvd.
Portland, OR

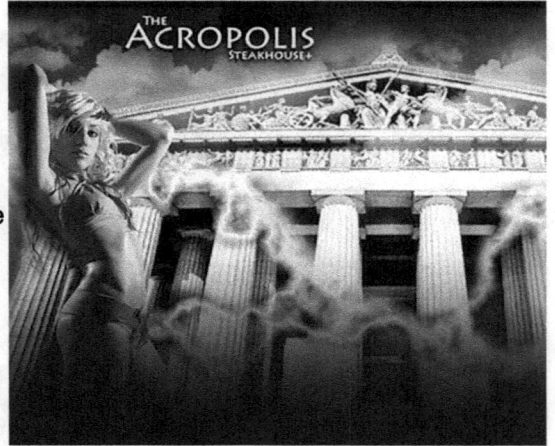

It isn't everyday that you drive by a building that is painted to resemble the country the owner is from. But that is what you see when you drive by one of Portland's nighttime landmarks, The Acropolis. The Acropolis, or known by as the A-Crop, is one of Portland's oldest Gentleman's Clubs.

Family owned and operated since 1976. The Acropolis is famous for many things, from having a large array of beer on tap, to four stages filled with some of Portland's most recognized and sought-after dancers, to its renowned selection of steak at a very reasonable price.

The Acropolis currently has 65 different types of beer on tap and sells its famous steak bites from morning till night. The infamous steak bites, steak special, and secret steak sauce draw crowds from all over the country with regular customer's making sure to swing by when they are in town. Previous customers contact The Acropolis regularly requesting a t-shirt with the famous statue of Zeus that has become the unofficial logo of the A-Crop. The delicious food even attracted an editor from the New York Times that notably wrote a small article regarding the reasonable price of such great tasting steak.

The Cheetah Lounge

Midtown, Spring at 8th
Atlanta, GA

The Cheetah, the Southeast's most renowned gentlemen's club and home of the legendary CheetahGirls - the most beautiful women in the South, performing nude.

The Cheetah caters to the highest expectations in adult entertainment, and has welcomed thousands of conventioneers, businessmen and devoted local customers for more than 40 years. Couples and female guests are frequent visitors, and The Cheetah has embraced a growing Atlanta population of young professionals and nightlife aficionados.

The heart of The Cheetah is its Main Room, the showcase for hundreds of beautiful CheetahGirls performing nude on three stages, on lighted tabletops, on bar-tops, and tableside.

The main room is flanked by two 25-foot bars each facing a lighted stage. At its center is floor seating with lighted tabletops facing the Main Stage runway. On both sides of main stage are special seating areas: To the

By Mike Enemigo

left, The Mezzanine, slightly removed and elegant table seating; To the right, Alluvia Restaurant for fine-dining during your visit.

Main Room guests enjoy high-def , big screen TV's, a state of the art sound & light system, and (on weekend nights) the high-energy of electronic dance music.

For a more cozy environment, may they suggest the Executive Room? All the hedonistic delights of The Cheetah presented in elegant comfort, just a few steps away from the buzz and excitement of the Main Room. The Executive Room is a quiet enclave of overstuffed chairs and sofas, a dedicated bar and service staff, and an atmosphere conducive to intimate conversations and cozy companionship. When you visit the Executive Room, imagine yourself hosting a private gathering in this space, comfortably seating up to 100 with a banquet area and gourmet buffet prepared by Alluvia Restaurant. See a manager to ask about reserving the Executive Room.

Immediately left of The Cheetah's main stage is The Mezzanine, only slightly removed from main room activity, The Mezz offers comfortable upholstered leather chairs and overlooks the main stage and Main Room entertainment.

Club Lit
35-35 Steinway St.
Queens NY11101

Lit Gentlemen's Club Queens – Club Lit Queens Astoria Queens newest and hottest strip club has burst onto the scene like wild fire. Lit NYC features an array of beautiful woman daily and can not be matched in its pure beauty. Lit Queens come equipped with a state of the arts sound system and over 4 stages to captivate your night the way it should be done.

Club Lit will exceed all expectations. There are many reasons why this Astoria hot spot is popular around Queens Natives. The bottle prices at Club Lit are very reasonable and Lit Strip Club guests get placed in VIP for the entire night unlike others that like to turn over tables. Club Lit is clean and well put together and the Club Lit hosts are extremely professional and friendly. Club Lit Queens NYC's policy is that guests are well cared for. As for the Lit NYC dancers, well lets just say they are very sexy and very talented. Lit Queens closely screens to make sure that they are top notch.

Devils Point

5305 SE Foster Rd.
Portland, OR 97206

At Portland's rock 'n' roll strip club, pints of Pabst are $2.00 and IPA and micro drafts are $4.00 and under , while Jack-and-cokes run $6.00. Tall tables, bar stools and standers are clothed in red and lit with oil lamps, and red carpeting covers the floor. Spot lighting glows Lucifer red. Sexy strippers grace the chain-suspended stage while eager patrons enjoy the views.

This friendly bar has everything you need: lascivious ladies, video poker and world class DJs that bump everything from Hank Williams to MIA. Bottled beer runs from New Castle to Sol, rounded out with domestics along with a wide variety of spirits. Sit at the bar and you'll never miss anyone entering or exiting. Picnic tables line the outside of the bar for smokers while strippers and karaoke singers collaborate every Sunday for world-famous Stripparaoke.

E11even

29 NE 11th St.
Miami, FL 33132

An immersive adventure encompassing the luxury and sophistication of a one-of-kind Ultraclub, E11EVEN MIAMI is entertainment reimagined.

The only 24/7 Ultraclub in Florida, E11VEN MIAMI is the winner of the prestigious "Best New Concept" award, as well as making the "Top 10 Clubs" by Nightclub & Bar, and the "Top 100 Clubs" by DJ Magazine, stabilizing its presence as one of the most sought after venue for both public and private events alike.
E11EVEN MIAMI is centrally-located in the heart of downtown, just blocks from Wynwood, the American Airlines Arena, Brickell, and minutes from South Beach. This $40 million award-winning landmark destination seamlessly operates as a nightclub and after-hours experience. The 20,000-SF space is perfectly designed to entertain and entice.

Surrounded by state-of-the-art lighting and sound, the club features 600 square foot of LED video walls and intelligent lighting, as well as the newest "Funktion-One" Resolution 6 sound system, the perfect backdrop for the club's Cirque-style performances, aerialists, choreographed go-go dancers and exotic acts. This high energy social playground plays host to an ever-growing roster of the entertainment industry's biggest names like Drake, Jamie Foxx, P Diddy, Jenny McCarthy, Donnie Wahlberg, Brody Jenner, as well as world-renowned DJs such as Diplo, Skrillex, DJ Snake, and Carnage. The most modern accouterments blend with five-star hospitality, premium bottle service, and a delectable food menu, and are all offered in an alluring environment that is as sexy as it is sophisticated.

By Mike Enemigo

The Executive Club
603 West 45th St.
New York, NY 10036

Featuring 10,000 square feet of opulence, Executive Club showcases the finest entertainers around the globe, the top-rated cuisine of Robert's Steakhouse, and the premiere setting for discerning clientele seeking the zenith in adult entertainment. The entertainment complex, which accommodates 400 guests, is designed with a two-story atrium which allow sweeping views from anywhere in the club. The showroom offers three high-octane performance stages and exclusive "backstage" bottle and Champagne service, as well as two additional sky stages suspended 20 feet above the floor. Their second level is home to Robert's Steakhouse, a fine dining restaurant which has received rave reviews from the New York Times and numerous other national publications. Also on this level are the exotic Harem Rooms, available for more intimate performances. For the VIP, they have exclusive Suites which can accommodate groups from 4-40. For guests seeking discretion, there is even an elevator leading to a hidden dining room.

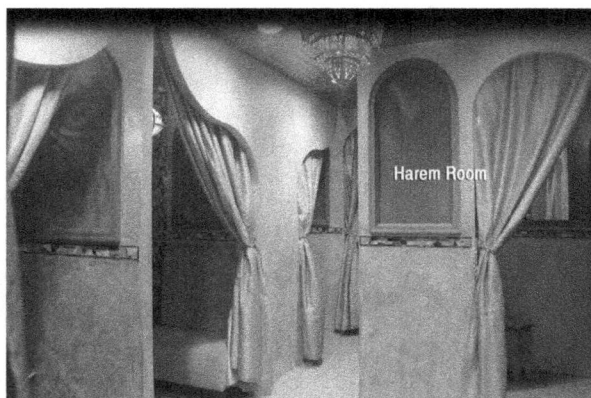

Private Room- Red Room

Harem Room

King of Diamonds
17800 Ipco Rd.
Miami, FL 33162

Atlanta might be Strip City, but KOD is the king of strip clubs, and rightfully so. Almost every rapper, from 2 Chainz and Gucci Mane to Lil B and Nelly, has mentioned this Miami nudie mecca in a song or two. Or three. Or four.

Boasting a roster of up to 100 girls, a dozen super sky boxes, 30 plus private VIP suites, a shoe shine station, a clothing boutique, a barber shop, tanning beds, full body massages, an auto detailing service, wi-fi/computers in the bathrooms... and a full food and drink menu, this cavernous spot is the king of strip clubs, at least if you listen to literally all the rappers and are a fan of all the athletes who show up on the regular.

KOD
GENTLEMENS CLUB
MIAMI

The Lodge
10530 Spangler Rd.
Dallas, TX 75220

The Lodge is America's best-known and most-honored gentlemen's club, setting the national standard for elegance, beauty and integrity since 1996. A spectacular edifice of timber and stone that seems straight out of the Rocky Mountains, The Lodge is nationally renowned for superb cuisine, unparalleled hospitality and enticing entertainers from around the world. The dancers - who are a minimum of 21-years old - also compete for an annual college scholarship, and put actual effort into their stage shows, which include acrobatics, fire juggling, and live snakes and happen on six stages on busy nights. That's all while you chow down on actually-delicious food from chef Jose Luis Nieto.

Penthouse Club
727 Iberville St.
New Orleans, LA 70130

If you're looking for typical New Orleans strip clubs, there are plenty to choose from. But why subject yourself to anything less than the absolute finest? Instead, treat yourself to the luxurious experiences available only at The Penthouse Club.

The Penthouse Club embodies both the wild nature of Bourbon Street and the sophistication of a gentlemen's club, all in one location. Their stunning, vivacious women and refined ambience provide the premier strip club experience.

With two full bars, two lavish floors, three stages crafted specifically for the visitors' entertainment, and state of the art lighting and sound, you can turn your experience at The Penthouse Club into anything you desire. They have a diverse range of amenities that cater to any style of night, including junior executive suites, exclusive penthouse suites, and unparalleled, private executive suites. They also offer superior tableside bottle service with your choice of almost any spirit imaginable.

The Penthouse Club provides the nightlife New Orleans locals and visitors alike crave. Whether you're hosting a bachelor party or relaxing with friends, they go above and beyond all other New Orleans strip clubs. At The Penthouse Club, they'll show you that perfection is possible.

Sapphire NYC
333 E 60th St.
New York, NY 10022

Sapphire New York is bringing premier adult entertainment to New York City, with the elegance and class as its sister club in Las Vegas. Sapphire

New York, the only gentlemen's club on the Upper East Side, offers deluxe amenities including designer suites with private butlers, concierge services and varying themes to satisfy every indulgence. With 10,000 square feet of space, 8,000 lovely ladies on staff and all the VIP amenities you could dream of, Sapphire New York is sure to make every man's fantasies come true.

Scores
26-50 BQE West,
Woodside, NY 11377

Located in Woodside NY, Scores Queens is Nightclub and Event Space. It features a unique decor and has it's own distinct personality and flavor. They have state of the art sound and audio offering all types of music including Hip-Hop, R&B, House and Rock & Roll. From corporate occasions to club nights, product launches to conferences, fashion shows to film shoots and showcases to concerts, Scores Queens is dedicated to providing the best in entertainment on every level. Check out Scores Queens for the best adult entertainment near LaGuardia Airport. They have multiple VIP rooms for private lap dances. They are the premiere Strip club in Queens NY. NYC Gentlemen's Club is now Scores Queens.

Spearmint Rhino
49-09 25th Ave.
Woodside, NY 11377

A cross between a nightclub and an upscale topless bar, the Rhino's always packed, especially on weekends."The waitresses are pleasant, not pushy, and the environment is super mellow," says Dan Hippler, strip-club reviewer for Vegas.com. "Lots of guys go there for business meetings or just to grab a drink after work."Spearmint Rhino has been named Best Strip Club twice by Las Vegas Weekly.

Starlets
49-09 25th Ave.
Woodside, NY 11377

Starlets isn't what you would imagine in this new era of strip clubs looking like state of the art party zones. Starlets is still the old-school gentlemen's den sort of club. Dark walls, most of the club is about the stage. You are never too far from a pretty girl when you are in Starlets. They have some of the best strippers Queens has to offer. This should be expected when their wait staff have launched themselves into mini celebrities. Starlets is the "day job" for some of the game's well-recognized video girls and urban models. The regular line up of bartenders have been renamed the Startenders. These girls bring in a regular celebrity clientele and big boy spenders. How can they not? This set of waitresses and bartenders are famous in their own right as well. Flip through a magazine or MTV/BET and you will run across one of them sooner or later. Starlets is the place where you step your game up before you walk through the door. Bring some money with you... some girl will be happy to motivate you to spend it.

Stateline Showgirls
6727 W Seltice Way
Post Falls, ID 83854

So, here's a clever way to get around those pesky "no nudity and liquor" laws: straddle your bar on a state line, so the booze is served in one state while the strippers dance in the other. That's exactly what they've done at Stateline, where you can go to the Washington side to watch completely naked dancers, then mosey back into Idaho for a cheap drink.

St. Venus Theater
21st St. and 6th Ave
New York, New York

The St. Venus Theater is an art, music and performance inspired erotic venue. They are an exclusive club, theater and lounge, always striving to be unique and exciting "one of a kind" utopia.

They claim they are many things, but not a strip club, a burlesque revival show, a swingers event, or a fetish party. They want to excite ones heart, mind, soul and libido, not just the libido. With a wide variety of erotic performances that are always a tribute to the woman and female sexuality.

Also featuring the most erotic and physically transformative lap dance you're likely to have ever known.

The St. Venus Theater is surely nothing you've ever experienced before.

By Mike Enemigo

Treasures Gentlemen's Club and Steakhouse

2801 Westwood Dr.
Las Vegas. NV 89109

There are many Las Vegas strip clubs, but only one is "The Most Luxurious Gentlemen's Club in the World." Treasures Las Vegas is truly the most opulent and comfortable adult entertainment venue in Las Vegas. From the moment you walk through the front entrance and into our dazzling ultra lounge, you immediately realize you are in the Mecca of entertainment for gentlemen in Las Vegas. Unbelievable, beautiful, opulent, warm, comfortable, unparalleled service and amenities- these are but a few ways to describe Treasures and the truly remarkable world into which you have stepped. They invite you to find out and experience all that a real gentlemen's club can be.

Treasures Gentlemen's Club & Steakhouse is one of the hottest clubs in Las Vegas and an experience not to be missed. They've spared no expense in creating the most enjoyable, luxurious, and intimate gentlemen's club in the world, as seen on Cinemax, E. Entertainment Television, and the Travel Channel.

Clubhouse
2250 Manana Dr
Dallas, TX 75220

There are 50 or so clubs in the Dallas/Fort Worth area, but as a two-time winner of Exotic Dancer Magazine's Nude Club of the Year, Clubhouse is the best.

"This is one of those places that has everything," says Texas stripper Susan Wayward. "Any type of girl you want, they have." The Clubhouse was also a favorite spot for members of Pantera. In fact, Vinnie Paul hosts a weekly Rock Band competition.

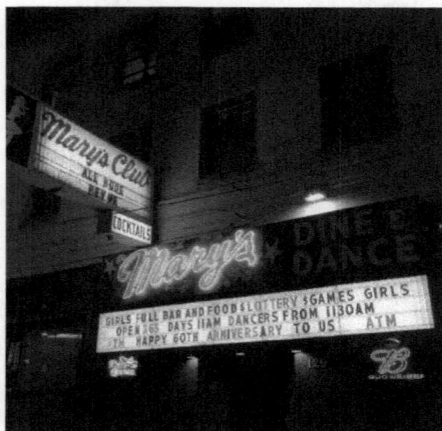

Mary's Club
129 SW Broadway
Portland, OR 97206

Visit this neon landmark for its vintage blacklight murals, hot nude girls, and relaxed, hole-in-the-wall vibe. Forty years after Roy Keller turned Mary's into Portland's first topless bar, his daughter slings drinks and a granddaughter gyrates on stage.

"It's not a high-pressure environment at Mary's," remarks Wayward. "It just feels like a party."

By Mike Enemigo

Lollipops Gentleman's Club

643 N Grandview Ave
Daytona Beach, FL 32118

What is the Lollipops motto? "Every place else sucks!" And while that may or may not be true, this NASCAR-circuit and spring-break mainstay has earned its place on our list. It's got three stages, a roster of 150 uber hotties (although no longer topless thanks to a heartless city ordinance), and a client list that includes Evel Knievel, Wesley Snipes, and Dale Earnhardt Jr. among others.

Sam's Hofbrau

1751 E. Olympic Blvd.
Los Angeles, CA 90021

This workingman-style watering hole with its 25 brands of beer, pool tables, and red-brick walls may leave you thinking hofbrau is German for hottie.
Stop by on Mon-days for $2 Coors Light and booty-shaking babes, all of whom are gorgeous but tough as nails. Take Isabella, for example. "She's originally from Queens and doesn't take crap from anybody," says Z-Bone, our friendly professor of stripper-ology.
"Sam's dancers wear their 'tude on their sleeves," he says, "but considering that's all they've got on, for them it works."

Strip Clubs

Kitty Kat: Adult Entertainment Non Nude Resource Book

89

Magic City
6241 Forsyth St. SW
Atlanta, GA 30303

GQ has called Magic City in Atlanta, "America's most important club" because of its ability to make or break a star in the hip-hop world. Dancers and patrons alike ultimately serve as the perfect baometer for whether a particular song can cut through the chaotic environment and truly make people want to get up and move. "You get the finest females in the state of Georgia," a patron told GQ. "You get the Who's Who of the streets in here. You can have Young Thug, Feature, 2 Chainz in here on the same night. And you get DJ Esco. If Esco play your record...? Everything Esco touches out here is off the charts." Little Magic, the manager of the club paints a vivid picture of what it's like to party at Magic City, saying, "gorgeous strippers, money everywhere and hot wings. It's not a strip club if you don't have money on the floor with hot wings on it.

Pirate's Cove
984 County Road 500 E
Portland, OR

"Not the only jug you'll see." A strip club that is oddly shaped like a jug. Located at 74th and N.E. Sandy the Pirate's Cove has been a landmark in Portland for the last 80 years. We have Keno, Video poker, and live DJ's everynight! Feel free to smoke and drink again AT THE SAME TIME on our new Smoking Patio! Our knowledgable bar staff and great exotic dancers make The Pirate's Cove the most friendly, fun exotic dance club ever. We look forward to meeting you!

By Mike Enemigo

Climax
6241 Forsyth St. SW
Atlanta, GA 30303

The drive-thru window at the Climax Gentleman's Club offers the novelty of a drive-thru tree with the I'll-do-it-in-my-car convenience of a drive-thru McDonalds. A special gravel driveway leads to a cinder block carport at the back of the building, where patrons can watch the indoor activity from their vehicles, through a diamond-shaped window. A "pay here" booth takes credit cards, and displays an autographed photo of Fred "The Honzman" Honsburger, a right-wing radio talk show host. Current rates are $20 a minute for two or more people; $10 a minute for solo customers. If there's someone in front of you, you just have to wait in your car.

Pure Gold's Crazy Horse
300 McCann St.
Nashville, TN 37210

There is a theory out there that the relative attractiveness of a city's female population is inversely proportional to its strip club talent. And nowhere does this prove truer than in Nashville, where the best strip club only garners 3.5 stars despite a city loaded with hot women; in fact, more reviewers tout the club's BYOB policy. Still, if you're in Nash-Vegas for a bachelor party, you can't beat full nudity and your own booze.

Devil's Point
300 McCann St.
Portland, OR

While Mary's might have made the opening credits of Portlandia, this article isn't called "The Strip Club You'd Find in the Opening Sequence of a Quirky Sketch Comedy Show." The award in Oregon goes to Devil's Point, where the crew of laid-back dancers not only hold summer-long bikini car washes, but they'll also walk your dog (not a euphemism) and strip while you sing karaoke (Stripperoke!).

Kitty Kat: Adult Entertainment Non Nude Resource Book

School House
984 County Road 500 E
Negoa, IL 62447

Admittedly, a town that only boasts a population of 1,600 people doesn't exactly scream "strip club bucket list" like other burgs in Las Vegas, Atlanta and Miami. However, the School House actually exists inside a former elementary school - making it one of the stranger strip clubs in the United States.

Once home to the Pioneer School - which for more than 50 years served as both a place of learning and a community center where people gathered to sing hymns, attend 4-H meetings and sell homemade pies - the school was sold in 2002 for $36,800 USD. The former cafeteria now features a small stage with a mirrored backdrop set that includes two stripper poles under black lights and the teachers lounge has been converted into a VIP room. In keeping with the school theme, the "Golden Rules" include, "Keep hands off dancers" and "No Hard Liquor."

The unassuming strip club school type venue boasts a hot pink buss out front with a sign in it's window "School House Bikini Club" as well as one that says "Bikini's, Cold Beer, Great Whiskey."

The club has caught quite the buzz and was even featured in the Chicago Tribune for it's small town having an issue with a school being turned into a strip club. See below.

Neighbors Upset Downstate School Has Been Converted to a Strip Club
by Steve Schmadeke, Tribune Reporter
Nancy Ward isn't happy about what's become of Pioneer School, which served for more than 50 years as both a place of learning and a community center where people gathered to sing hymns, attend 4-H meetings and sell homemade pies.
About six months ago, the vacant elementary school bordered by homes on a rural highway was converted into a strip club called The School House. Downstate residents are still fuming.
"It's a whorehouse," said Ward, co-owner of a nearby garden center where she and her husband live. "I honestly don't feel as safe here as what I did. And the name they gave it; that is unbelievable. There's nobody in there learning anything, I guarantee you."
The school about 60 miles south of Champaign was sold by the Neoga school district in 2002 for $36,800. Now, three nights a week, as many as 10 topless dancers perform in the former cafeteria on a small stage with a mirrored backdrop set that includes two stripper poles under black lights.
The teachers lounge has been converted into a VIP room where lap dances go for $20, an ATM installed outside. The walls are hung with multiplication tables, chalkboard, a history of U.S. presidents and a poster titled "Class Rules" that reads "Keep hands off dancers." One entrance has been fenced off for a smoking area, and a sign near the back door reads "No Hard Liquor."
"Myself, I wished it was gone and the hell out of here," said Frank Enloe, 74, a former sheriff's deputy who has lived about 300 feet north of the school since 1965. Now he doesn't feel comfortable hosting late-night cookouts

By Mike Enemigo

on his patio and wakes each night as the club lets out around 2 a.m. "It bothers us ; we put all five of our children through here."

"It just makes us sick," said Marian Lindley, a former teacher at the school.

But to Bob Kearney, a union electrician who runs the club with business partner Travis Funneman, The School House is a legal business that has been a small bright spot for the county's economy.

It doesn't serve alcohol and has never been cited by authorities, and only one person has been arrested there; for damaging club property. For those seeking such entertainment, the other nearest venues are more than an hour away.

"This building was falling apart; we totally renovated it," said Kearney, who has a one-year lease on the former school. "Nobody cared about this building until we moved in. You show me another business in Cumberland County that has created 30 jobs for people.

"It's no longer an argument of legality; now it's an argument of morality," he said as a stripper crawled across the stage. "Is this Nazi Germany? Are they the Taliban? It's OK to break the laws as long as it's in the views of my religion?"

There were no adult-business regulations in Cumberland County before the club opened, and it remains the only such business in the county. To obtain what amounts to a business license, the owners in September wrote their names, addresses and business name in an old leather-bound county book and ran a newspaper ad for three weeks.

They were not required to say what type of business they had planned.

As talk of what was going on in the schoolhouse spread, the county in December prohibited adult businesses from opening within 1,000 feet of homes, schools or parks. It also banned completely nude performances.

But the owners say the law doesn't apply to existing businesses, and at least for now, county authorities apparently agree.

Still, the County Board has commissioned a study to determine if the new ordinance would illegally ban any strip club from the county, a first step in possible legal action.

"This is a very small county, and the people just don't want it," said County Board Chairman Robert Swearingen. "They don't want this in their neighborhood, and I can't really say I blame them."

Strip clubs are afforded protection under the First Amendment, and officials realize they could potentially be walking into a legal minefield by attempting to force The School House to close.

"You can't make it a witch hunt," said Cumberland County State's Attorney Barry Schaefer. "You can regulate adult businesses, but if you can't regulate it the right way, it won't hold water in court."

Residents here have happily lived alongside other sometimes-noisy organizations, such as the Central Illinois Motorcycle Club and the bar that opened in an old church up the road.

But even if it's legal, many residents remain fiercely opposed to a strip club, run by out-of-towners, in what many still consider their school in the heart of their crossroads community.

A small number of protesters still gather each night across the street, light a bonfire and post a sign that says, "Does your family know where you are? Jesus does."

A Neoga church's bulletin includes a prayer request each month for "changed hearts at the Old Pioneer School."

Protester Nadine Kastl, 81, a retired school bus driver for Pioneer School, recalled how at a recent basketball game an opposing team's fans waved dollar bills at the Neoga cheerleaders, apparently in reference to the new strip club.

"I can't believe that happened to our kids," she said.

Dancers interviewed at the club said they viewed the old schoolhouse as just another workplace, though the protesters were something new.

Residents are encouraged by what many say has been a drop in business at The School House since it opened, and they are hopeful it quietly will go away. Kearney, though, still has big plans.

"The classrooms; eventually we would like to make them theme rooms and do bachelor parties and private parties," he said. "But that can wait. They didn't build the Taj Mahal overnight."

Mirage Exotic Nightlife
6430 Burnt Poplar Rd.
Greensboro, NC

The only club in the state to land a 5-star Yelp review. This place not only has hot dancers and killer food specials ($2 Taco Tuesdays, $4 steaks on Wednesdays, etc), but if you're showing up with six or more dudes, they'll send a limo for you, ABSOLUTELY FREE.

Bare Exposure
2303 Pacific Ave.
Atlantic City, NJ 08401

The BYOB full-nude strip club may be the single greatest innovation to come out of the state of New Jersey. OK, it definitely is. And nowhere is it cooler than at this spot near the Trump Tower, which, despite charging a "cell phone holding fee", hires the hottest (fully nude) strippers in AC and even lets you get on stage with two of them (only $35!) for a special "hot seat" dance.

Downtown Cabaret
115 S. 4th Street
Minneapolis, MN 55401

The top-rated spot in the Twin Cities has one of the more impressive strip club interiors you'll see anywhere, with high ceilings reminiscent of a gilded-era train station, a library themed room, and an entrance that looks like it should have sorority letters out front. The place is so impressive that strip club connoisseur Mike T. from Minneapolis said, "WOW!!! This is hands down the best gentlemen's club I have ever set foot in, and I've been to a few!!" And by a few, we think he means every stripper in Minneapolis knows his face.

By Mike Enemigo

PT's Showclub
200 Riverside St.
Portland, ME

It would be pretty disappointing to hear all this great stuff about Portland strip clubs, make your way up to Maine, and then realize you were in the wrong Portland. About the only way to salvage your trip would be to head here, a newly-renovated space that's part of the PT's family of clubs and absolutely nothing like the vegan/stripperoke establishments you'd find in the Beaver State.

Shotgun Willie's
490 Colorado Blvd.
Glendale, CO

"The Best Show Club in Denver" is a completely open 10,000 sq. ft. room with eight stages but zero VIP areas. Which may be disappointing if you were looking for "extras" from one of the 200 beauties roaming the floor. But what they lack in VIP space they more than make up for in glass-enclosed, state-of-the-art conference rooms you can reserve for official business meetings.

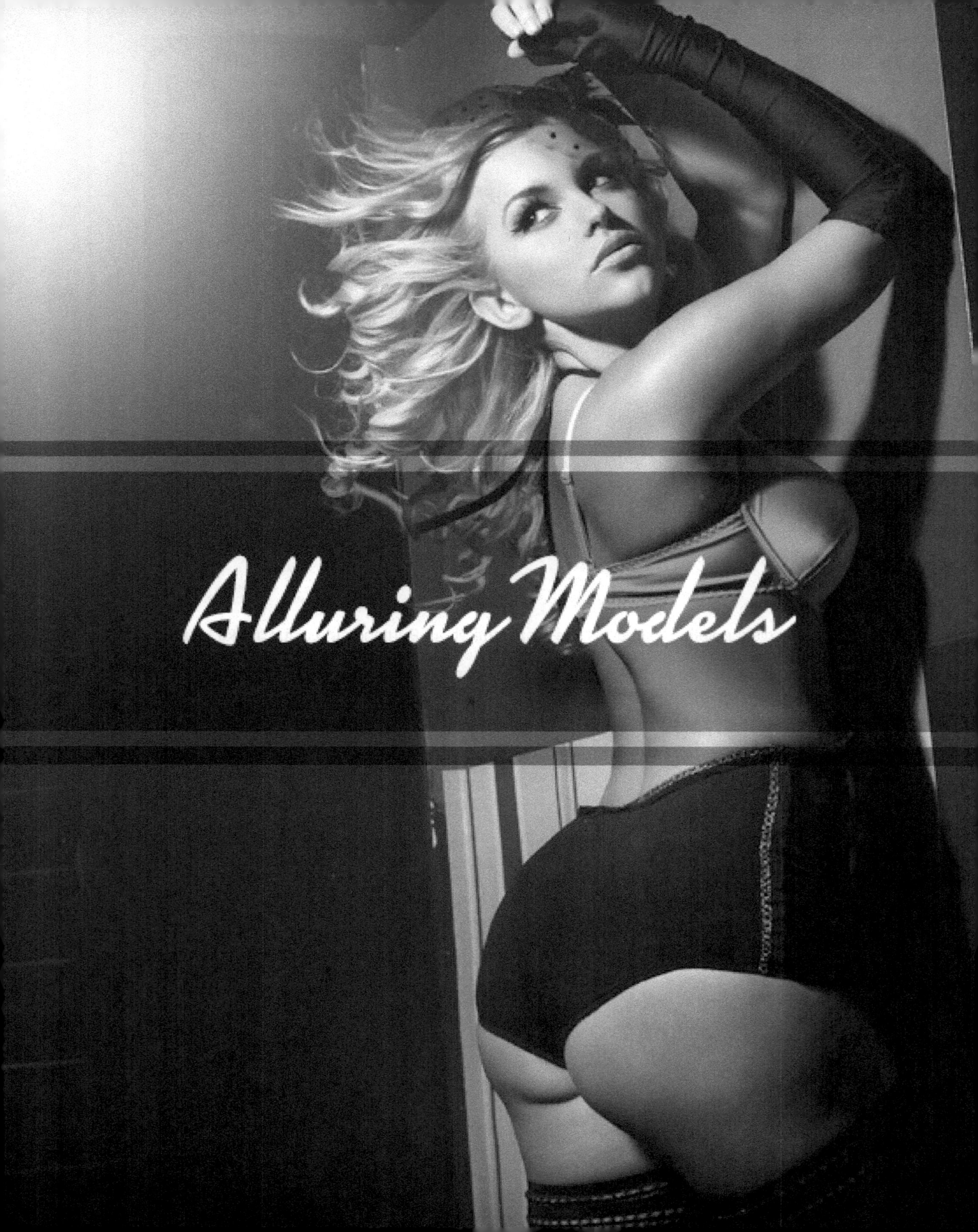
Alluring Models

MODELS

Below are names and addresses of some of the hottest models in the world, and/or their agencies. Though you are never guaranteed a response, often you can write, mention that you are a huge fan, and request that they send you a picture or fan club packet. Hey, you're in prison, so it's worth a shot, right?

Alden, Ginger
25 Rolling Hill Ct. W.
Sag Harbor, NY 11963

Aldridge, Lily
184 Thompson St., Apt. 5
New York, NY 10012

Alves, Camila
c/o Jesse Parker Stowell Full
Picture Management
915 Broadway, Floor 200
New York, NY 10010

Ambrosia, Alessandra
2314 La Mesa Dr.
Santa Monica, CA 90402

Austin, Coco
8125 River Rd., Apt. 68
North Bergen, NJ 07047

Bledel, Alexis
c/o Paul Brown
New Wave Entertainment
2660 W Olive Ave.
Burbank, CA 91505

Burke, Brooke
4320 Mar iota Ave.
Toluca Lake, CA 91602

Bush, Lauren
c/o Staff Member
Elite Model Management
245 5th Ave., Floor 24
New York, NY 10016

Campbell, Naomi
c/o David Unger; Resolution
1801 Century Park E, Ste. 2300
Los Angeles, CA 90067

Canalis, Elisabetta
c/o Staff Member; Corsa Agency
11704 Wilshire Blvd., Ste. 204
Los Angeles, CA 90025

Crawford, Cindy
33246 Pacific Coast Hwy
Malibu, CA 90265

Curry, Adrianne
425 N Sycamore Ave., Apt. 8
Los Angeles, CA 90036

Curry, Adrianne
c/o Chris Kelly
Marilyn Model Management
32 Union Sq. E
New York, NY 10003

De La Cruz, Rosie
Wilhelmina Models
300 Park Ave. 5, #200
New York, NY 10010

Derek, Bo
PO Box 1940
Santa Ynez, CA 93460

D'Errico, Donna
4365 Hillview Dr.
Malibu, CA 90265

Evangelista, Linda
c/o Didier Fernandez DNA Model
Management
555 W 25th St., Floor 6
New York, NY 10001

Flavin, Jennifer
30 Beverly Park
Beverly Hills, CA 90210

Hasselhoff, Hayley
c/o Liz Anderson
Lisa Anderson P.R.
8060 Melrose Ave., Floor 4
Los Angeles, CA 90046

Herzigova, Eva
c/o Scott Lipps; One Management
42 Bond St., Apt. 2
New York, NY 10012

Hilton, Paris
3340 Cleredon Rd.
Beverly Hills, CA 90210

Huntington-Whiteley, Rosie
c/o Jeff Speich Anonymous Content
3532 Hayden Ave
Culver City, CA 90232

Iman
285 Lafayette St. #7DE
New York, NY 10012

Janssen, Famke
c/o Emily Gerson Saines Brookside Artists Management
250 W 57th St., Ste. 2303
New York, NY 10107

Jenner, Kendall
25115 Eldorado Meadow Rd.
Hidden Hills, CA 91302

Jenner Kylie
c/o Kance Klein
William Morris Endeavor
9601 Wilshire Blvd.
Beverly Hills, CA 90210

Kerr, Miranda
c/o Aleen Keshishan
Brillstein Ent. Partners
9150 Wilshire Blvd., Ste. 350
Beverly Hills, CA 90212

Kinski, Nastassja
1110 Bel Air Pl
Los Angeles, CA 90077

Klum Heidi
3384 Stone Ridge Ln.
Los Angeles, CA 90077

Krupa, Joanna
1425 Brickell Ave., Apt. 42C
Miami, FL 33131

Kurkova, Karolina
c/o Scott Lipps; One Management
42 Bond St., Apt. 2
New York, NY 10012

Alluring Models

LeBrock, Kelly
PO Box 57593
Sherman Oaks, CA 91413

Lepore, Amanda
c/o Bill Coleman, Peace Bisqult
963 Kent Ave., Apt. E3
Brooklyn, NY 11205

Lima, Adriana
c/o Chris Kelly
Marilyn Model Management
 32 Union Sq. E, PH
New York, NY 10003

Linkletter, Nicole
c/o Staff Member
Elite Model Management
245 5th Ave., Floor 24
New York, NY 10016

Lombard, Karina
EOS Entertainment Corp.
1209 N Orange St.
Wilmington, DE 19801

Lynch, Kelly
c/o Tiffany Kuzon
Evolution Entertainment
901 N Highland Ave
Los Angeles, CA 90038

Macpherson, Elle
c/o Michael McConnell Maverick
Artists Agency
6100 Wilshire Blvd., Ste. 550
Los Angeles, CA 90048

Madison, Holly
3626 Regal Pl.
Los Angeles, CA 90068

Michelle, Candice
c/o Jerry Donato
Abraxis Talent Agency
4260 Troost Ave., Apt. 1
Studio City, CA 91604

Moakler, Shanna
3890 Prado De La Mariposa
Calabasas, CA 91302

Moynahan, Bridget
c/o Andrea Pett
Joseph Brillstein Ent. Partners
9150 Wilshire Blvd., Ste. 350
Beverly Hills, CA 90212

Nelson, Colette
PO Box 1122
Seaford, NY 11783

Nemcova, Petra
c/o Michael Samonte
Sunshine, Sachs
8409 Santa Monica Blvd.
West Hollywood, CA 90069

Nielsen, Brigitte
3374 Floyd Terr.
Los Angeles, CA 90068

Paradis, Vanessa
7760 Woodrow Wilson Dr.
Los Angeles, CA 90046

Phillips, Bijour
2151 Hollyridge Dr.
Los Angeles, CA 90068

Phillips, Busy
Mosaic
9200 West Sunset Blvd., 10th Floor
Los Angeles, CA 90069

Randall, Anne
10526 W. Tropicana Dr.
Sun City, AZ 85351

Reece, Gabrielle
c/o Lisa Shotland
Creative Arts Agency
2000 Ave.s of the Stars, Ste 100
Los Angeles, CA 90067

Refaeli, Bar
c/o Scott Lipps; One Management
42 Bond St, Apt. 2
New York, NY 10012

Rhoda, Hilary
c/o Staff Member; 1MG Models
304 Park Ave S., Fl. 12

Seymour, Stephanie
385 Iaconic Rd.
Greenwich, CT 06831

Shields, Brooke
36 Lewis St.
Southampton, NY 11968

Sims, Molly

43 S. Breeze Dr.
East Hampton, NY 11937

Smalls, Joan
c/o Vanessa Gringer
1MG Models
304 Park Ave S., Fl. 12
New York, NY 10010

Swanepoel, Candice
c/o Liz Carpenter; 1MG Models
304 Park Ave S., Floor 12
New York, NY 10010

Tanaka, Aiko
PO Box 1025
Beverly Hills, CA 90213

Tiegs, Cheryl
9663 Santa Monica Blvd., #339
Beverly Hills, CA 90210

Turlington, Christy
c/o Lisa Jacobson
United Talent Agency
9336 Civic Center Dr.
Beverly Hills, CA 90210

Tweed, Shannon
2650 Benedict Canyon Dr.
Beverly Hills, CA 90210

Upton, Kate
c/o Ilene Feldman
LBI Entertainment
2000 Ave.s of the Stars Floor 3,
North Tower
Los Angeles, CA 90067

Ward, Gemma
c/o Staff Member
Caliber Media Company
5670 Wilshire Blvd., Ste. 1600
Los Angeles, CA 90036

Williams, Edy
PO Box 6325
Woodland Hills, CA 91365

Wilson, Torrie
525 Woods Landing Trail
Oldsmar, FL 34677

Zucker, Arianne
4226 Babcock Ave
Studio City, CA 91604

By Mike Enemigo

Camila Alves

Brooke Burke

Coco Austin

Lauren Bush

Alessandra Ambrosia

Alexis Bledel

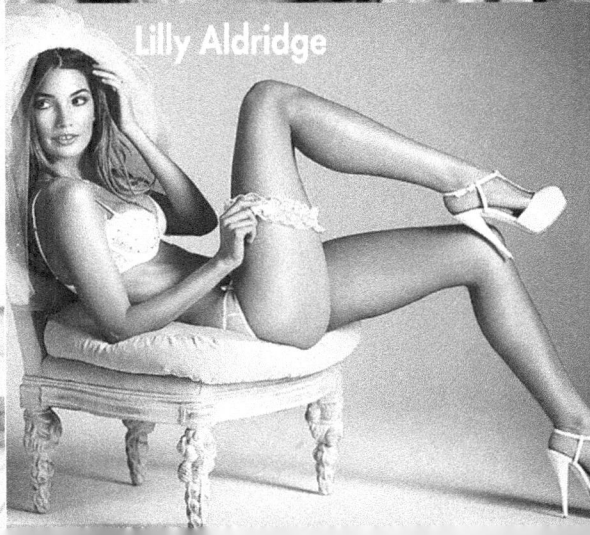
Lilly Aldridge

Ginger Alden

Adrianne Curry

Rosie De La Cruz

Cindy Crawford

Jennifer Flavin

Donna D'Errico

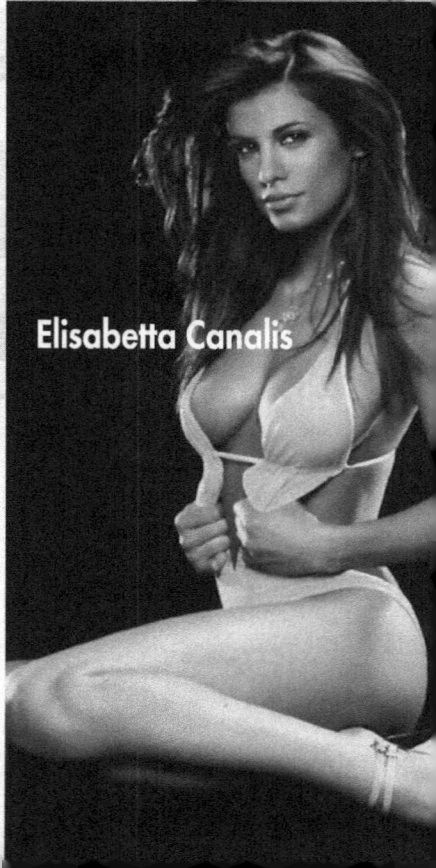

Elisabetta Canalis

Naomi Campbell

Bo Derek

Eva Herzigova

Miranda Kerr

Linda Evangelista

Paris Hilton

Hayley Hasselhoff

Famke Janssen

Iman

Rosie Huntington-Whiteley

Kendall Jenner

Nastassja Kinski

Kylie Jenner

Joanna Krupa

Andriana Lima

Karolina Kurkova

Heidi Klum

Shanna Moakler

Candice Michelle

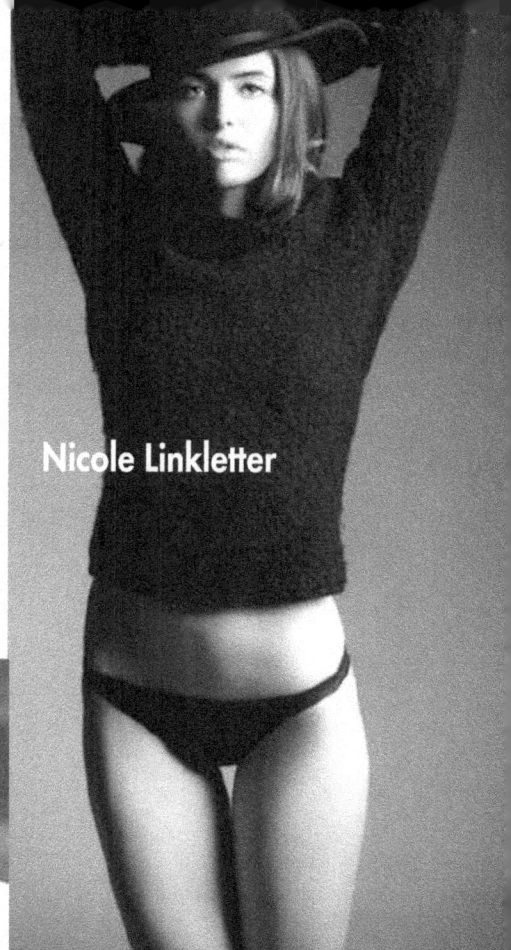

Nicole Linkletter

Elle Macpherson

Holly Madison

Amanda Lepore

Kelly Lynch

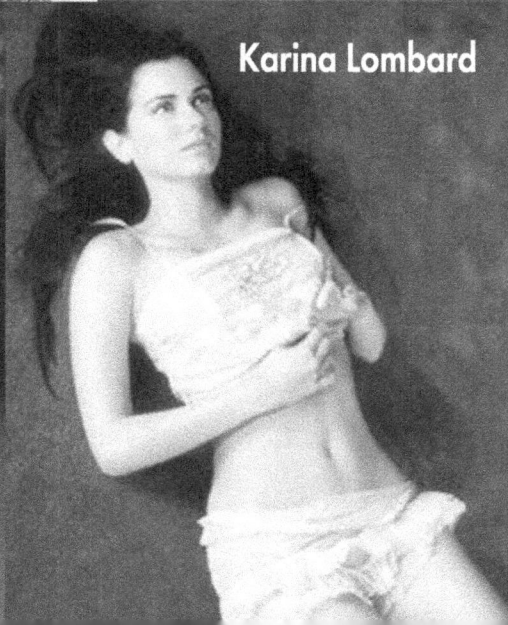

Karina Lombard

Gabrielle Reece

Brigitte Nielsen

Petra Nemcova

Bijou Phillips

Colette Nelson

Bridget Moynahan

Busy Phillips

Vanessa Paradis

Bar Refaeli

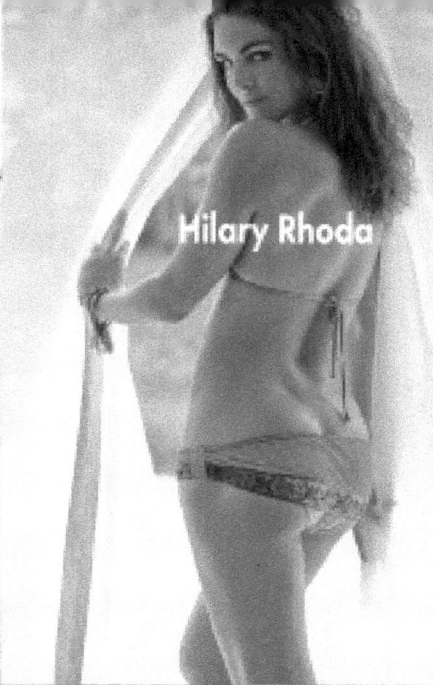

Hilary Rhoda

Brooke Shields

Stephanie Seymour

Molly Sims

Joan Smalls

Aiko Tanaka

Candice Swanepoel

Arianne Zucker

Shannon Tweed

Christy Turlington

Kate Upton

Gemma Ward

Edy Williams

Cheryl Tiegs

Torrie Wilson

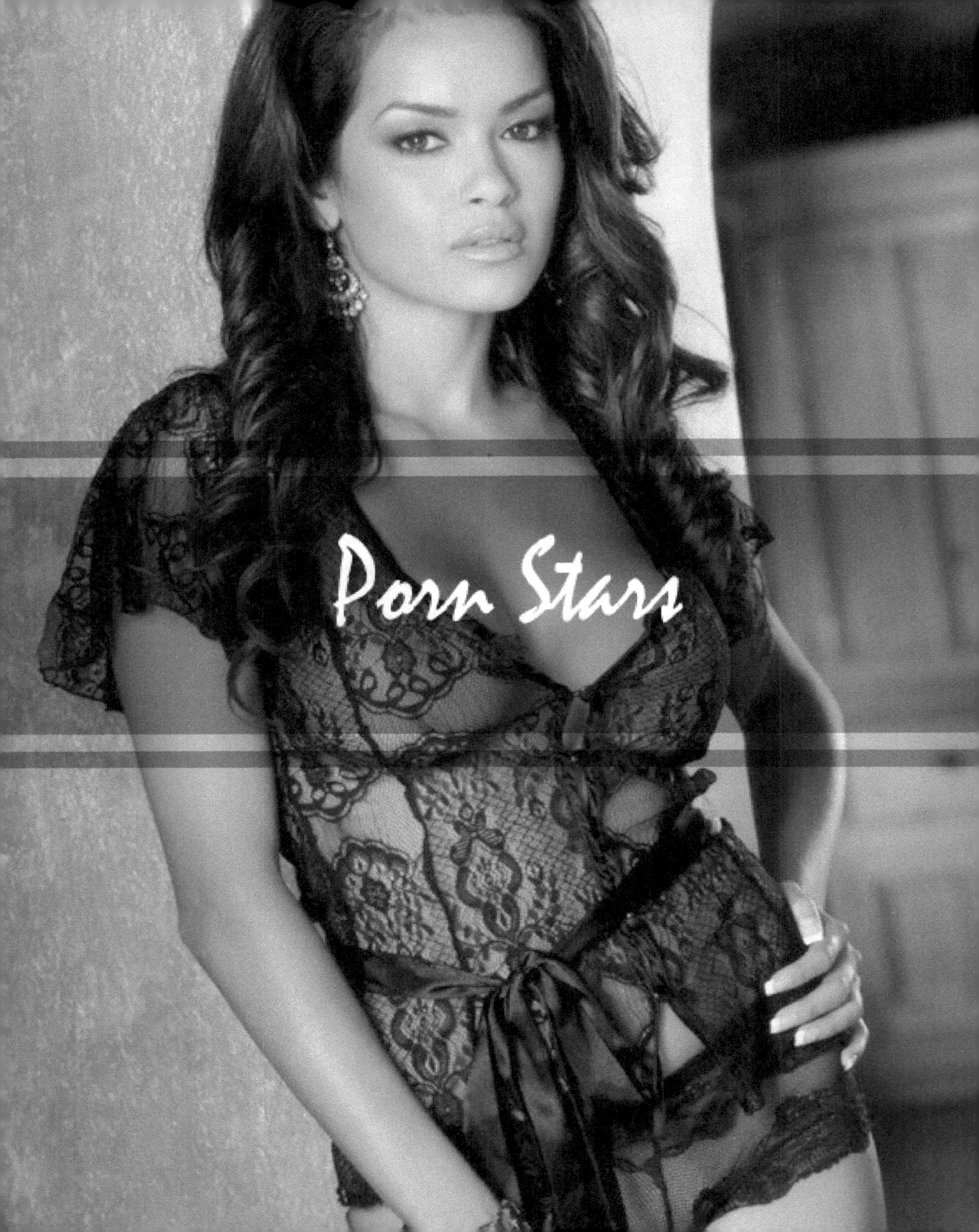
Porn Stars

Aidra Fox

BIRTHDATE: September 25, 1995
HOME TOWN: Milwaukee, WI

HEIGHT: 5ft 7in
WEIGHT: 125 lbs
MEASUREMENTS: 32C-28-34 in

CAREER: Aidra is a hard-core porn star who features in lesbian, anal, masturbation, solo, group, and other sex videos. Basically anything sexual and Aidra is involved. She has created a big name for herself in her short career so far.

TRIVIA:
First time anal in Anal POV Style, HardX.com, August 08, 2014
Tattoos: woman and a rose on upper back; rose on right hip; writing on inside left wrist

AWARDS:

AVN Awards 2015: Best Boy/Girl Sex Scene Jean Fucking (2014), shared with Ryan Madison

MOVIES:

✪ Aidra Fox profile at ATK Premium
✪ Brazzers Network Aidra Fox (multi-site pass)
✪ Digital Desire Aidra Fox (babe and pornstar
        pictures & movies)
✪ Digital Playground Aidra Fox (porn star movies)
✪ Aidra Fox profile at Kink
✪ Aidra Fox profile at Mofos Network
✪ Naughty America Aidra Fox (multi-site pass)
✪ Aidra Fox at Nubiles Reality Kings Aidra Fox (multi-site pass)
✪ Twistys Aidra Fox (babe pictures & movies)
✪ Woodman Casting X Aidra Fox (casting movies)
✪ Ztod Aidra Fox (Zero Tolerance Studio porn movies)

London Keyes

BIRTHDATE: August 18, 1989
HOME TOWN: Seattle, WA

HEIGHT: 5ft 4in
WEIGHT: 130 lbs
MEASUREMENTS: 34D-27-36
NUMBER OF ADULT FILMS:

CAREER: After appearing in several Jonni Darkko movies, he produced a movie around her, L for London. She performed her first anal scene in this movie with Manuel Ferrara and Asa Akira.

AWARDS:
✪ 2010 AVN Award nomination for Best New Starlet
✪ 2011 XBIZ Award Nomination for Web Babe of the Year
✪ 2012 AVN Award Nomination for Best Oral Sex Scene in L for London

MOVIES:

✪ Teens With Tits, 2008
✪ Bounce, 2009
✪ Addicted to Boobs, 2010
✪ Don't Tell My Daddy You Fucked My Big Titties
✪ No Rest for Big Breasts, 2012
✪ 1000 Facials London Keyes (facial movies, part of My XXX Pass)
✪ Ass Parade London Keyes (big ass movies, part of Bangbros Network)
✪ Aziani London Keyes (babe movies & pictures)
✪ Baby Got Boobs London Keyes (big tits movies, part of Brazzers Network)
✪ Bangbros London Keyes (multi-site pass)
✪ Big Butts Like It Big London Keyes (big butt porn star and huge cock movies, part of Brazzers Network)
✪ Big Mouthfuls London Keyes (cum swallowing movies and pictures, part of Bangbros Network)
✪ Big Tit Cream Pie London Keyes (part of Bangbros Network)
✪ Big Tit Cream Pie London Keyes (part of Bangbros Network)
✪ Big Tit Cream Pie London Keyes (part of Bangbros Network)
✪ Big Tits at School London Keyes (big tit movies, part of Brazzers Network
✪ London Keyes sets at In The Crack
✪ London Keyes profile at Kink
✪ Naughty America London Keyes (multi-site pass)
✪ Reality Kings London Keyes (multi-site pass)
✪ Real Wife Stories London Keyes (wife stories movies, part of Brazzers
✪ Rodney Moore London Keyes

Anya Ivy

BIRTHDATE: January 28, 1992
HOME TOWN: Atlanta, GA

HEIGHT: 5ft 2in
WEIGHT: 110 lbs
MEASUREMENTS: 36D-29-38

CAREER: Gorgeous, buxom, and shapely 5'2"
black knockout Anya Ivy was born on January
28, 1992 in Atlanta, Georgia. Ivy spent her
summers in Florida while growing up and lost
her virginity at age fourteen. Moreover, Anya was
a competitive cheerleader who graduated from
high school with honors. Ivy attended college
for two years before she began performing in
explicit hard-core fare at age twenty-two in 2014
after meeting a woman who was established
in the porn industry in her hometown of Atlanta
who introduced Ivy to her agent. Among the
various adult websites that Ivy has worked for are
BangBros, Brazzers, Mofos, Team Skeet, ATK
Exotics, Reality Kings, Casting Couch X, Foot
Fetish Daily, and New Sensations.

MOVIES:

✪ Baby Got Boobs Anya Ivy, Brazzers Network
✪ Big Tits at Work Anya Ivy, Brazzers Network
✪ Bit Tits at School Anya Ivy, Brazzers Network
✪ Brazzers Network Anya Ivy (Multi-Site Pass)

Montana Fishburne

BIRTHDATE: August 17, 1991
HOME TOWN: Unknown

MEASUREMENTS: 34D-25-36

CAREER: Released in early August 2010 by the studio Freaky Empire, the gonzo porn film Phattys Rhymes & Dimes 14 features an almost hour-long sex scene between Fishburne and porn actor Brian Pumper. Fishburne later attempted to block the distribution of the film. Her legal team contacted Pumper, whom she claims leaked the rehearsal footage which was never intended to be released.

She performed again in the film Montana Fishburne: An A-List Daughter Makes her XXX Debut, released on August 10, 2010 by Vivid Entertainment. The film is over an hour long and features Fishburne in a car, a hotel room and a shopping mall. Commenting on why she decided to make the film, she said, "I view making this movie as an important first step in my career ... I've watched how successful Kim Kardashian became and I think a lot of it was due to the release of her sex tape by Vivid." Fishburne says she is in talks with Vivid about signing a multi-picture deal due to the initial commercial success of her debut.

She revealed that her father is "very hurt" about her porn career, and initially stated that she believed he would eventually view it as a positive. She later stated that he had cut ties with her and that she was "no longer welcome in his life" due to her career choice.

LEGAL PROBLEMS:
Fishburne was arrested for prostitution in 2009. She reportedly cut a deal with prosecutors who dropped the solicitation and prostitution charges in exchange for her pleading no contest to misdemeanor criminal trespass and entering a work-alternative program.

In August 2010, Fishburne was charged by the L.A. City Attorney's Office with simple battery and false imprisonment when she allegedly broke into a woman's home, forced her into a bathroom and allegedly assaulted her.

TRIVIA:
Daughter of actors Laurence Fishburne and Hanja O. Moss.

By Mike Enemigo

Daisy Marie

BIRTHDATE: February 6, 1984
HOME TOWN: Los Angeles, CA

HEIGHT: 5ft 4in
WEIGHT: 130 lbs
MEASUREMENTS: 34D-27-36
NUMBER OF ADULT FILMS: 190+

CAREER: She has appeared in over 190 adult movies since 2002, made two special appearances on The Howard Stern Show (July 2003 and November 2004) and has posed for various adult magazines such as Chéri, and worked with photographers such as Suze Randall. Daisy Marie has also worked with Suze's daughter Holly Randall for the mainstream sports brand Fantasy Fitness. A sports enthusiast, she has shared that she's a "die-hard Laker fan" with AIP Daily. In 2005, she appeared in the controversial 50 Cent music video "Disco Inferno". Marie was one of the finalists on the second season of Playboy TV's reality competition show, Jenna's American Sex Star. She later hosted the Playboy TV series All Nite Party Girls. She has appeared in Hot Babes Doing Stuff Naked is a collection of 18 ten-minute segments currently airing on Playboy TV that showcase adult models and adult actresses doing various outdoor activities without clothing in public places. It's based on the Italian T.V. show S.O.S. Potata. Roughly five women are featured per episode, including Playboy TV regulars Erika Jordan, and Kate Brenner. No sex acts occur during any of the segments, just slow motion shots of various activities like horseback riding, roller skating, fishing, etc.

As of 2008 she was represented by the adult entertainment talent agency LA Direct Models. She appears on the cover of the June 2008 issue of Penthouse as well as being featured as the Pet of the Month.

PARTIAL FILMOGRAPHY:
✪ Busty Bonitas Bon Bons
✪ Milk Jugs
✪ Doubl D Divas

MOVIES:

✪ 1000 Facials Daisy Marie (facial movies, part of My XXX Pass)
✪ Aziani Daisy Marie (babe movies & pictures)
✪ Baby Got Boobs Daisy Marie (big tits movies, part of Brazzers Network)
✪ Ball Honeys Daisy Marie (Latina and black movies & pictures, part of Bangbros network)
✪ Ball Honeys Daisy Marie (Latina and black movies & pictures, part of Bangbros network)
✪ Ball Honeys Daisy Marie (Latina and black movies & pictures, part of Bangbros network)
✪ Bang Bus Daisy Marie (reality porn movies, part of Bangbros network)
✪ Bangbros Daisy Marie (multi-site pass)
✪ Big Mouthfuls Daisy Marie (cum swallowing movies and pictures, part of Bangbros Network)
✪ Big Mouthfuls Daisy Marie (cum swallowing movies and pictures, part of Bangbros Network)
✪ Big Tits at Work Daisy Marie (big tit movies, part of Brazzers Network)
✪ Big Tits Boss Daisy Marie (big tits movies, part of Reality Kings)

Christy Mack

BIRTHDATE: May 9, 1991
HOME TOWN: Chicago, IL

MEASUREMENTS: 34DD-24-36

CAREER: Christy Mack started her modeling as a tattoo model. Besides photo shoots for mainstream magazines Rebel Ink, Inked Girls and she also did photos for the websites Brazzers and Bangbros. As an actress, she appeared in the 2010 Independent splatter film Zombie Abomination: The Italian Zombie Movie - Part 1. In 2012, she started her career in the American porn industry starring in a number of films such as Hot Body Ink produced by Elegant Angel, Whores Ink and Inked Angels produced Evil Angel and Inked Girls produced by Wicked Pictures, Mack also played the role of Zatanna in the movie The Dark Knight XXX - A Porn Parody from Vivid Entertainment.

On December 19, 2012, R&B singer Rihanna posted an Instagram photo of Christy Mack on Twitter that showed Mack's butt. This was commented by Christy Mack: That's me, only the butt tattoo was photoshopped on, It's beeb circulating for a while in 2013, Mack starred in Digital Playground's Shortcut which also featured main stream stars Bibi Jones and Tommy Gunn.

In the fall of 2013, it was announced that Mack would star in the film Rambone: A Dream Zone Parody, a porn parody of the Rambo films the studio Dream Zone Entertainment. It was also the first time that she worked for European production company on camera. Magma Film shot with her the film Porn in the USA, which was published in the autumn of the same year. In July 2013, the studio Wicked Pictures produced the porn movie "Wanderlust" directed by Stormy Daniels featured Mack in the largest sex scene of her career along with 4 other actors.

MOVIES:

- ✪ Ass Parade (big ass movies, part of Bangbros)
- ✪ Baby Got Boobs (big tits movies, part of Brazzers)
- ✪ Backroom Facials (facial movies & pictures, part of Bangbros)
- ✪ Big Mouthfuls (cum swallowing movies and pictures, part of Bangbros)
- ✪ Big Tit Cream Pie (Part of Bangbros)
- ✪ Blowjob Fridays (blowjob movies, part of Bangbros)
- ✪ Brazzers Network (multi-site pass)
- ✪ Dorm Invasion (part of Bangbros)
- ✪ Naughty America (multi-site pass)
- ✪ Party of Three (three way movies, part of Bangbros)
- ✪ PAWG (big ass movies and pictures, part of Bangbros)
- ✪ Porn Star Spa (reality porn movies, part of Bangbros)
- ✪ Vivd Christy Mack (Vivid Porn Stars)

Ayana Angel

BIRTHDATE: June 28, 1976
HOME TOWN: Atlanta, GA

MEASUREMENTS: 36DD-23-26

CAREER: Ayana Angel was born in Atlanta, GA. Before becoming a porn star she was a stripper in Atlanta. Ayana earned her status in the porn biz the "hard" way. Like many adult entertainers she started off with stripping before doing smut videos, but unlike a log of her cohorts, she was able to get her Bachelors degree. If you have ever seen her movies, you might think that a diploma is for giving dome, getting hit from the back (pick a hole) and various other acts of perversion. Often cast as an insatiable MILF later in her career, Ayana got nude and crude with unashamed determination that always left her a sweaty, slimy mess at the climax of her scenes, something her fans loved her for.

MOVIES:

✪ 1000 Facials (My XXX Pass)
✪ 40 Ounce Bounce (Big Ass Movies)
✪ Ass Parade (Big Ass Movies)
✪ Ball Honeys (Latina and black movies and pictures, part of Bangbros)
✪ Bangbros
✪ Bootylicious (Big Ass Movies)
✪ My First Sex Teacher (MILF reality movies, Naughty America)
✪ Score Videos (Big Tit Movies)
✪ Porn Mega Load (HD Videos)

Katsuni

BIRTHDATE: April 9. 1979
HOME TOWN: Lyon, Rhone-Alpes, France

MEASUREMENTS: 32D-25-33

CAREER: Katsuni has won 28 awards in both Europe and the United States. She works both in France and Los Angeles. She has won four anal sex awards, including the 2004 "Best Anal Sex Scene" NINFA award at The International Erotic Film Festival in Barcelona, and three AVN "Best Anal Sex Scene" awards in 2004, 2005, and 2006. Some of her other awards include "Best Foreign Couple Scene" (2003 and 2004), "Best Lesbian Scene" (2004), "Best Tease Performance" (2006), and "Best Actress" (10 awards). In the beginning of 2007 she signed an exclusive contract with Digital Playground. During that time she also received breast implants.

Katsuni has appeared in Penthouse magazine. She originally went by the stage name Katsumi, but she was barred by a French judge in January 2007 from using that name after a woman named Mary Katsumi sued due to the closeness to her own name. In October 2007 Katsuni was fined 20,000 euros for violations of the ban on using the name "Katsumi". Katsuni has recently undergone a breast augmentation to size DD breasts.

On August 14, 2013, Katsuni announced that she was retiring from porn in order to focus on her acting career.

MOVIES:

- ✪ Pirates II : Stagnetti's Revenge (Digital Playground)
- ✪ MILFs Seeking Boys (Reality Junkies)
- ✪ Club Katsuni (Premium Pass)
- ✪ 21 Sextury (multi-site pass)
- ✪ Bangbros
- ✪ Big Tits at Work (big tit movies)
- ✪ Big Tits in Uniform (big tits movies, Brazzers Network)
- ✪ Club Sandy (babe movies and pictures)
- ✪ Diabolic (Diabolic Studio Porn Movies)
- ✪ Digital Playground (porn star movies)
- ✪ Hustler Katsuni (Hustler movies and pictures)
- ✪ Jizz Bomb (facial movies, part of NS All)

By Mike Enemigo

Diamond Monroe

BIRTHDATE: November 30
HOME TOWN: Unknown

MEASUREMENTS: ??-51-??

CAREER: Diamond Monroe has started in categories such as Natural Tits, Car, Titty-fucking, Face Fuck, Cum-ass Facila, Hairy, Hot Babes, Pool Shaved, Lesbians, Blowjobs, Bubble Butt, Interracial, Cream Pie

MOVIES:

✪ Ass Parade 50
✪ Brown and Beautiful (Reality Kings)
✪ Brown Bunnies 14 (Bang Productions)
✪ DearLorenzo.com 10 (Platinum Pictures)
✪ Platinum Collection (Platinum Pictures
✪ Wet Black Ass Overload (West Coast
    Productions)

Kandi Kream

BIRTHDATE: April 16, 1983
HOME TOWN: Fresno, CA

MEASUREMENTS: 36DD-34-44

CAREER: Kandi Kream is a former American adult model and porn star. Many of her films featured her large ass, and anal sex. She's also known for lesbian scenes and her luscious chest. She shot an anal scene with male co-star Ace in a very small trailer where the two barely had room to move around. Her shoots have primarily been with black men and she uses her bountiful breasts to bring male co-stars to climax.

MOVIES:

✪ Fuck My Tits 1(Elegant Angel)
✪ Black and Natural Big Boobs (Totally Tasteless)
✪ Ass Parade (Big ass Movies)
✪ Big Wet Butts (Big Ass Movies)
✪ Bootylicious (Big Ass Pictures)
✪ Brazzers Network (Multi-Site Pass)
✪ Busty Fever (Big Tits Movies)
✪ Plumper Pass (Multi-Site Pass)
✪ Round and Brown (ebony movies and pictures - Reality Kings)
✪ TugJobs (handjob movies and pictures, Bangbros)

By Mike Enemigo

Kylee Kross

BIRTHDATE: January 1
HOME TOWN: Cuba

MEASUREMENTS: B34
HEIGHT: 5'5"
PIERCINGS: Nipples; Clithood; Snakebites; Filtrum; Right nostril

CAREER: Kylee Kross was born Nicole Pettas. She is an actress.

MOVIES:
- ✪ Cum On My Tattoo
- ✪ The XXXorcist
- ✪ Guide 2 Humping
- ✪ P.O.V. Punx
- ✪ Deep Inside Joanna Angel
- ✪ Joanna Angel's Alt Corruption
- ✪ One On One 5
- ✪ Untamed Sex Acts 4

Carter Cruise

BIRTHDATE: April 24, 1991
HOME TOWN: Cary, North Carolina

HEIGHT: 5ft 4in
WEIGHT: 121lb
MEASUREMENTS: 34C-25-37in
NUMBER OF ADULT FILMS: 176

CAREER: Carter Cruise began working as an erotic model in the summer of 2013. She made her porn debut in August of the same year after contacting the Florida based talent agency East Coast Talents. She moved to Los Angeles in March of 2014 and signed with Spiegler Girls in June. That same month she was featured in AVN's "fresh" issue.

Cruise has appeared in several features, including "Mrs. Polito" in American Hustle XXX from Smash Pictures and as a stepsister in Cinderella XXX. She was cast as the lead in director Jacky St. James' romance , Second Chances.

TRIVIA: In 2015, Cruise became the second performer to ever win AVN Awards for Best New Starlet and Best Actress in the same year, after Jenna Jameson in 1996.

AWARDS:

✪ Best Actress, Second Chances
✪ Best New Starlet, AVN
✪ Best Three-Way Scene, Facialized 2

MOVIES:

✪ Brazzers Network Carter Cruise (multi-site pass)
✪ Diabolic Carter Cruise (Diabolic studio porn movies)
✪ Digital Playground Carter Cruise (porn star movies)
✪ Hustler Carter Cruise (Hustler movies & pictures)
✪ Carter Cruise profile at Kink
✪ New Sensations Carter Cruise
✪ Penthouse Carter Cruise
✪ Reality Kings Carter Cruise (multi-site pass)
✪ Wicked Pictures Carter Cruise
✪ Cruise (Zero Tolerance Studio porn movies)

By Mike Enemigo

Tera Patrick

BIRTHDATE: July 25, 1976
HOME TOWN: Great Falls, Montana

HEIGHT: 5ft 9in
WEIGHT: 121lb
MEASUREMENTS: 36E-24-38

CAREER:

Tera was discovered by a talent scout for the Eileen Ford Modeling Agency, and at the age of 13 she was signed to a contract to be a model. She moved to New York City shortly thereafter and her career as a runway and catalog model began. At 18, she left the world of modeling and enrolled at Boise State University where she received her associate's degree in nursing and a bachelor's degree in Microbiology.[She then transferred to University of California, Santa Barbara, where for financial reasons she began modeling again.

In the late 1990s, Tera began appearing in nude and softcore features. In 2000, she made the transition to hardcore porn in Andrew Blake's Aroused. She has since appeared in more than seventy adult features.

Tera was Penthouse magazine's Pet of the Month for February 2000 and was selected as "Pet of the Year" runner-up. She also appeared on the cover and in a pictorial in the March 2002 issue of Playboy. Tera was the publisher of Genesis magazine, a popular men's magazine, beginning in 2003. She appeared on the cover of seven issues of the publication.

Tera was featured on the cover of the July 2006 edition of the mainstream magazine FHM. Tera, who had been named one of FHM's 100 sexiest women, was the first porn star to appear on the cover. She was also a sex columnist for FHM (U.K.) from 2003 to 2008.

In 2010, Tera's memoir, Sinner Take All, was released, and she starred in the (non-porn) Indonesian horror film Rintihan kuntilanak perawan ("The Moaning of the Virgin Ghost")

AWARDS:

✪ F.A.M.E. Award: Favorite Female Starlet
✪ AVN Hall of Fame Inductee
✪ Genesis Magazine: Porn Star of the Year 2008

MOVIES:

✪ Welcome to Boobstown, Pleasure Productions 2009
✪ Hustler Tera Patrick (Hustler Movies)
✪ Mr Skin Tera Patrick (celebrity movies and pictures)
✪ Pornstar Legends Tera Patrick (retro pornstar)
✪ Penthouse Tera Patrick (Penthouse pictures & movies)
✪ Sexy Babes Tera Patrick (babe/hardcore pics & movies)
✪ Vivid Tera Patrick (Vivid porn stars)
✪ Digital Desire Tera Patrick (babe & pornstar movies)

Dani Daniels

BIRTHDATE: September 23, 1989
HOME TOWN: Orange County, California

MEASUREMENTS: 34C-24-37

CAREER: Daniels began stripping before her porn career to pay her rent. Her stage name was derived from the first name of an ex-boyfriend as an act of revenge against him. She entered the adult film industry in January 2011, joining the agency OC Modeling. Her first scene was for Reality Kings. She was initially a lesbian-only performer, but later started performing with men. Her first four sex scenes with me were in the film Dani Daniels: Dare for Elegant Angel. Daniels was the Twistys Treat of the Month for July 2011, the Penthouse Pet of the Month for January 2012 and Elegant Angel's Girl of the Month for March 2014. That same month, Brazzers cast her in the lead role of a five-part series title The Whore of Wall Street, an adult parody.
She has gone on to perform for the 2014 film Dani Daniels Deeper, which won the AVN Award for Best Interracial release and the XBIZ Award for Interracial Release of the Year in 2015. In 2015 she collaborated with Doc Johnson to create a lineup of sex toys, which won the 2016 AVN Fan Award for Most Amazing Sex Toy. Daniels was placed on CNBC's list of "The Dirty Dozen: Porn's Most Popular Stars" in 2014 and 2015.

AWARDS:

✪ XBIZ Award for Interracial Release of the Year
✪ The Dirty Dozen: Porn's Most Popular Stars in 2014 and 2015
✪ 2013 Best Girl/Girl Sex Scene
✪ 2015 Best All-Girl Group Sex Scene
✪ 2015 Best Solo/Tease Performance
✪ 2015 Best Three-Way Sex Scene - G/G/B
✪ 2016 AVN Fan Award for Most Amazing Sex Toy

MOVIES:

✪ Brazzers Network Carter Cruise (multi-site pass)
✪ Filly Films
✪ Penthouse Studios
✪ Reality Kings

By Mike Enemigo

Halle Hayes

BIRTHDATE: February 9, 1988
HOME TOWN: San Jose, CA

HEIGHT: 6' 0"
WEIGHT: 136
MEASUREMENTS: 36DD-27-38
NUMBER OF ADULT FILMS: 30+

CAREER: Halle is smart and intelligent and has the manners of a true lady. She is well-spoken, calm, and has a great sense of humor. Halle said that she fucked around 50 guys before she entered the adult industry, which unequivocally means that experience is on her side. She has an awesome sense of stage performance that she achieved dancing in clubs of California. She started her porn career in the second half of 2019 when she was 21, and when she signed for 101 Modeling Agency. So far, she appeared in at least 19 solo, lesbian, and hardcore scenes. Halle discovered masturbation when she was quite young. Since then, she says she masturbated at least once a day. In her opinion, masturbation is the perfect way for stress relief. When she does it, she usually thinks about someone eating her pussy. She likes to use different sex toys and always has a lot of fun. Halle filmed one lesbian scene so far, and she let us know how much she loves eating pussies. The scene was filmed with an experienced September Reign. The fact that she is submissive always turns her on. Every command or suggestion that she gets from her partner she executes with pleasure. Practicing yoga for years, her body became so flexible that allows her to make a split in both ways and do the most challenging sex positions. Her favorite sex position is reverse cowgirl. It allows her to control the fucking and she thinks people like to watch her pussy wide open. She loves swallowing and facials. She always considered cream pies as rewards. She simply likes the feeling of a pulsating cock in her cunt. Halle is a great fan of anal sex and does it pretty often in her personal life. So far, she worked with some of the most famous actors such are: Charles Dera, Danny D, Jordi El Nino Polla, Lucas Frost, Manuel Ferrara, Prince Yahshua, Ryan Madison, Sam Cox, Scott Nails, Steve Holmes, Zac Wild, etc. Halle worked for studios such as Brazzers Network, Reality Kings, Devil's Film, Girlfriends Films, 5K Porn, D&E Media Networks, Jules Jordan Video, Dogfart Network, Mile High, Kelly Madison Networks, etc. Halle perceives the porn industry as modern art and a perfect job.

MOVIES:

- ✪ All Black X
- ✪ Deeper
- ✪ Glory Hole Initiations
- ✪ Round and Brown

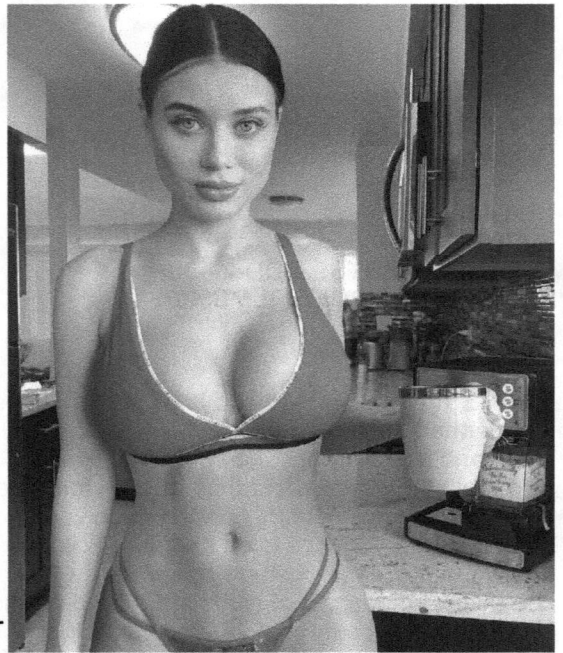

Lana Rhodes

BIRTHDATE: September 6, 1996
HOME TOWN: Chicago, IL

MEASUREMENTS: 34D-23-35
HEIGHT: 5'3"
WEIGHT: 120

CAREER: Lana shot her first hardcore scenes in April 2016 after moving from Chicago to Los Angeles and quickly became known to a wider audience. Her first scene was a solo scene for FTV girls in which she did a foot fetish and used a few sex toys. By August 2016, she was involved in about 50 porn productions. After a three-month break and the associated return to her hometown of Chicago, she is since November 2016 back in front of the cameras. Lana has worked for several of the world's premier production companies including Evil Angel, Jules Jordan Video, Tushy, Elegant Angel, and HardX. She was in the US edition of Penthouse magazine "Pet of the Month" in August 2016. In January 2017, Lana Rhoades was voted "Best New Starlet" at the XBIZ Award as well as the Audience Award "Hottest Newcomer" at the AVN Award. In March 2017, Lana Rhoades relocated to Los Angeles. In January 2018, she was presented with the AVN Award as part of the Adult Entertainment Expo in Las Vegas. From April to August 2016, Lana Rhoades worked for the Spieglergirls agency and from January to the beginning of October 2017, she was represented by LA Direct Models. Currently, she is not affiliated with a modeling agency. In 2019, Lana Rhoades was the most searched for porn star on Pornhub with more than 345 million views. She triumphed over second and third place stars Mia Khalifa and Riley Reid.

AWARDS:

- ✪ Fan Award: Hottest Newcomer (2017)
- ✪ Best Anal Sex Scene, Anal Savages 3 (2017)
- ✪ Most Popular Female Performer PornHub (2016)
- ✪ Porns Best Superstar Spank Bank (2017)
- ✪ Porn's It Girl Spank Bank (2017)
- ✪ XBiz Best New Starlet (2017)
- ✪ POV Perfectionist of the Year Spank Bank (2019)

MOVIES:

- ✪ Ultimate Fuck Toy
- ✪ Blacked (TV Series)
- ✪ Anal Beauty
- ✪ Lesbian Hookup
- ✪ Schools Out
- ✪ Big Wet Butts (TV Series)
- ✪ And many more!

By Mike Enemigo

Ayumi Anime

BIRTHDATE: October 17, 1989
HOME TOWN: Los Angeles, CA

MEASUREMENTS: 34C-25-32

HEIGHT: 5'7"
WEIGHT: 114 lbs

CAREER: Meet Ayumi Anime an American starlet with deep Korean roots, who is still getting tips in the adult entertainment industry. She was a mainstream model appearing in shoots for international fashion and sports brands such as Nike, Armani, and Chanel. She is born and raised in Los Angeles, and she has made it the base of her operations. The best thing about Ayumi Anime is that she is tattoo free and as a porn connoisseur, you will agree that her crossing over to the porn side of modeling has put a much-needed spotlight on Korean starlets is currently available to do girl-on-girl and solo scenes, and she brings sunshine to every set given that she is an eager babe and a people pleaser. She was the Penthouse Pet of the Month in October 2017. Despite being a newbie, she is comfortable being on camera, covering herself with oil, or flashing her tits on the beach. Ayumi Anime left the mainstream modeling and got into porn in 2017, and she has racked in an impressive following on social media. She has no chills about taking off her clothes and cozying up with a fellow starlet, yet her solo scenes are equally sensational. Despite sticking to a soft genre of porn, this starlet is aiming for the stars, and she is the undisputed oriental porn princess. Ayumi Anime has worked for various porn directors and production studios including many Vids, Cherry Pimps, Twistys Network, FM Concepts, Hustler Video, girlsway.com, Fantasy Massage, Brazzers Network, Jules Jordan Video, Girlfriend Films, Digital Sin, and Mile High. You can check out her fantastic nude photos on various porn forums, or check out her webcam videos on MyFreeCams from 7pm-1am LA time. However, she has unreleased scenes and you ought to follow her on social media to be among the first people to know when her new content is dropping. There has been much banter since her first scene dropped and despite what everyone had to say, she could care less. Ayumi Anime has made peace with her new career choice; her fans have encouraged her to keep going, having moved on from her past life. We hope that she keeps shooting and still doing her shows on her cam channel. The sky is the limit for this model.

AWARDS:

✪ Nominee: All-Girl Performer of the Year
✪ Nominee: Best All-Girl Group Sex Scene
✪ Nominee: Favorite Indie Club Star
✪ Nominee: Asian Empress of the Year
✪ Nominee: Tiniest Vag

MOVIES:

✪ Alum Asian Chick
✪ Anal Plug and Cum on Public Venice Beach
✪ Cheating Lesbian MILFs
✪ Cooling Down
✪ Double O
✪ & More!

Anna De Ville

BIRTHDATE: April 24, 1997
HOME TOWN: Portland, OR

MEASUREMENTS: 30DD-22-32
HEIGHT: 5'2"
WEIGHT: 99 lbs.

CAREER: The main reason she joined the industry is because she wanted to spend the summer after her 18th birthday in Europe. She had photo shoots in London and earned enough to pay for her European summer. After she went back home, she decided that she liked the industry and that she wanted to stay and work as a porn actress. She wasn't intimidated from her first scene at all. During the one year she is in the industry, she has learned a lot and improved herself and her positioning.

Anna considers herself to be a voyeur and an exhibitionist and loves public sex. Her family knows she does porn and they fully support her. In five years she still sees herself in porn and hopes to write an erotic novel one day.

AWARDS:

✪ Winner of Best Foreign-Shot All-Girl Sex Scene
✪ Nomine: Best Solo/Tease Performance

MOVIES:

✪ Double Penetration for Anna De Ville
✪ Bacchanalia
✪ Rocco's Time Master: Revenge of the Sex Witches
✪ Butthole Whores 7
✪ OMGape
✪ Elements
✪ Bound Gangbangs
✪ Everything Butt
✪ Fake Taxi
✪ Sit on My Face
✪ Throated
✪ Trashy Love Story
✪ Lesbian Adventures: Older Women, Younger Girls 11
✪ & More

By Mike Enemigo

Jessie Volt

BIRTHDATE: March 29, 1990
HOME TOWN: Bordeaux, France

MEASUREMENTS: 32B-24-36
HEIGHT: 5'1"
WEIGHT: 110 lbs

CAREER: Jessie became part of the adult film industry in 2010 when he was twenty years old. Being the ideal pocket Venus it wasn't a problem for her to land new parts once she her first shot for PixandVideo, part of the 21Sextury Network. She is represented by the agency Brill Babes in Europe and by the agent Mark Spiegler in the United States. So far she has worked with Penthouse, Twistys, Adam & Eve, Nubile Films, Glory Hole, Evil Angel, 21 Sextury, Babes Network, Harmony Vision, Jules Jordan Video, New Sensations, Interracial Blowbang and Digital Playground. Among this list of serious porn production and websites, she worked also with DDF Prod, Brazzers, Naughty America, Jules Jordan, Wicked Pictures and Reality Kings.

AWARDS:

✪ Galaxy Award 2012: Best European Performer
✪ AVN Award 2013 Female Foreign Performer of the Year

MOVIES:

✪ Slippery When Wet 2
✪ Box Truck Set
✪ Le Hard Corner
✪ Black Massive Cocks
✪ London Knights: A Heros & Villians XXX Parody
✪ Bitches Abroad 1: Foreign Pickups Hungary
✪ Cute White Girls Love Big Black Cocks
✪ Hard in Love
✪ Horney Hotties
✪ Big Wet Butts
✪ & More

Porn Stars

Nici Dee

BIRTHDATE: June 24, 1994
HOME TOWN: Praha, Czech Republic

MEASUREMENTS: 32C-24-36
HEIGHT: 5'1"
WEIGHT: 105 lbs

CAREER: Buxom and shapely 5'2" brunette knockout Nici Dee was born on July 4, 1993 in Prague, Czech Republic. Dee first started modeling nude in 2013. Among the notable adult websites Nici has worked are Nubiles, Met-Art, Foxes, Sex Art, and Photodromm. After being contacted by a Playboy photographer's assistant on Facebook, Dee did her first nude shoot for Playboy Plus in May, 2016 under the pseudonym Clara. Nici likes going to the spa in her spare time.

MOVIES:

- ✪ Babes
- ✪ Wow Girls
- ✪ In the Crack
- ✪ X-Art
- ✪ Hot Legs & Feet
- ✪ Nubiles
- ✪ Playboy Plus
- ✪ Fantasy Flirt

By Mike Enemigo

Ana Foxxx

BIRTHDATE: October 29, 1988
HOME TOWN: Rialto, CA

MEASUREMENTS: 34C-26-36
HEIGHT: 5'7"
WEIGHT: 130 lbs

CAREER: Gorgeous and slender 5'7" African-American stunner Ana Foxxx is the daughter of a minister who also served in the U.S. Air Force. A nerd during her high school days, Ana originally wanted to be a clown or a ballerina. After being discovered in a grocery store, Ana worked as a runway model prior to her involvement in the adult entertainment industry. Foxxx did her first hardcore shoot for the adult website Reality Kings. Among the notable companies Ana has appeared in X-rated features for are Adam & Eve, Evil Angel, Jules Jordan Video, and Pure Play Media. She was nominated for an AVN Award for Best New Starlet in 2013.

AWARDS:

✪ CherryPimps Cherry of the Month 2018

MOVIES:

✪ Pure Taboo
✪ Kinky Bites
✪ VR Bangers
✪ Lucky Seven
✪ Matriarch
✪ Lucky Seven
✪ Matriarch
✪ Black Cougars on the Prowl
✪ Deeper
✪ Lesbian PsychoDramas
✪ Bound Gangbangs
✪ & More

Lily Love

BIRTHDATE: December 11, 1991
HOME TOWN: Gulf Shores, AL

MEASUREMENTS: 34D-27--37
HEIGHT: 5'3"
WEIGHT: 125 lbs

CAREER: Lily Love was born in Gulf Shores on December 11, 1991 in the "The Yellowhammer State" of Alabama. The beautifully-figured 5' 3" brunette of German and Polish descent, began her adult entertainment career in 2012. Since then she has worked for numerous companies including Naughty America, Brazzers, Erotica X, Bang Bros, Reality Kings, Blacked, PornPros, Penthouse, Pure Passion and more. Lily is a multiple-time award nominee, including nominations by the 2013 Sex Awards for "Hottest New Girl" and "Porn's Best Body". In 2015, she was nominated by the XBiz Awards for "Best Actress in a Couples-Themed Release" for her work with Marcus London, Tyler Nixon and Dana DeArmond in The Escort 2 (2014).

MOVIES:

- ✪ Bang Bus
- ✪ Erotica X
- ✪ Lesbian Training Sessions
- ✪ Blacked
- ✪ WankzVR
- ✪ Dirty Masseur
- ✪ Racks Vol. 3
- ✪ Vixen
- ✪ The Darkest Shade
- ✪ Baby Got Boobs
- ✪ & More

130

Little Caprice

BIRTHDATE: October 26, 1988
HOME TOWN: Brno, Moravia, Czech Republic

MEASUREMENTS: 32B-25-34
HEIGHT: 5'1"
WEIGHT: 90 lbs

CAREER: Markéta Štroblova was born and spent her early years in the city of Brno, Czech Republic, where she graduated as a nutritionist. In 2008 she started her career in the adult industry after being discovered by the company Teenharbour. Working under the name of Little Caprice, she reached some degree of popularity that allowed her to have her own exclusive website of adult paid content. A petite brunette Caprice has done solo, lesbian and hardcore scenes since 2008, but she is also famous for nude glamour photography. She is currently living in Vienna, Austria.

AWARDS

✪   Twisty's Treat of the Month 2013
✪   Vixen Angel 2019
✪   AVN Award: Female Foreign Performer of the Year 2020

MOVIES:

✪   X-Art
✪   Russian Institute Lesson
✪   Nubile Films
✪   Blacked
✪   Vixen
✪   Metal Bondage
✪   Fakehub Originals
✪   Real Agent
✪   Anal Beauty 10
✪   & More

Darcie Dolce

BIRTHDATE: December 10, 1992
HOME TOWN: Sacramento, CA
MEASUREMENTS: 32E-23-33
HEIGHT: 5'2"
WEIGHT: 110 lbs

CAREER: Darcie Dolce is an Italian, German and American descent. She started her career in the adult entertainment industry in 2015 at the age of 23. She was named the Penthouse Pet of the Month in February 2016. She has appeared in over 130 films as an actress. Aside from her career as an adult film actress, Dolce also works as a DJ.

AWARDS:

- ✪ Penthouse Pet of the Month 2016
- ✪ Twisty's Treat of the Month 2016
- ✪ CherryPimps Cherry of the Month 2017

MOVIES:

- ✪ Booty Calling
- ✪ Girlsway Originals
- ✪ All Girl Massage
- ✪ Crushing on my Bestie
- ✪ Mommy's Daughter 2
- ✪ Sorority Rush Week
- ✪ Hot and Mean
- ✪ Lesbian Kissing 2
- ✪ & More

By Mike Enemigo

Viking Barbie

BIRTHDATE: October 22, 1985
HOME TOWN: San Antonio, TX

MEASUREMENTS: 36D-24-38
HEIGHT: 5'10"
WEIGHT: 145 lbs

CAREER: Kayleigh Swenson (aka Viking Barbie) was born in San Antonio, TX where she also grew up. Viking Barbie's full name is Kayleigh Megan Swenson. Viking Barbie's father's name is Robert Swenson, a professional wrestler who went by the name "Jeep Swenson" and remembered for portraying villain Bane in George Clooney starred 1997 film "Batman and Robin". He died later at the age 40.

Viking Barbie's mother, Erin Patricia Swenson, who herself was a moderately successful dancer and model. Kayleigh's parents got married in Bexar County, Texas. She is the only child of her parents.

She never disappoints her fans when it comes to flaunting her curvy figure of 40-26-40 inch onscreen. The Texas bombshell's Instagram account is loaded with sensuous and erotic photographs that one cannot miss. Viking Barbie's Height is 5 feet 10 inches and the Insta-fit-girl maintains a healthy weight of 145 lbs. Her natural hair color is blond and she has rare blue eyes.

MOVIES:

✪ Best in Sex: 2020 AVN Awards

By Mike Enemigo

SEXY GIRL PARADE
Prison Friendly Photo Book

SEXY GIRL PARADE
Prison Friendly Photo Book

See more in SEXY GIRL PARADE by GOLIATH BOOKS
Distributed by Freebird Publishers

PUBLISHED BY
GOLIATH

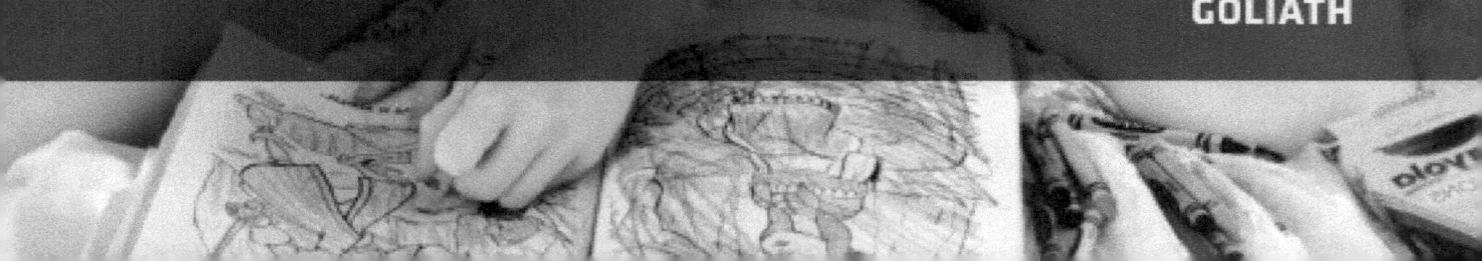

SEXY GIRL PARADE
Prison Friendly Photo Book

SEXY GIRL PARADE
Prison Friendly Photo Book

See more in SEXY GIRL PARADE by GOLIATH BOOKS
Distributed by Freebird Publishers

PUBLISHED BY
GOLIATH

SEXY GIRL PARADE
Prison Friendly Photo Book

See more in SEXY GIRL PARADE by GOLIATH Books
Distributed by Freebird Publishers

PUBLISHED BY
GOLIATH

SEXY GIRL PARADE
Prison Friendly Photo Book

See more in SEXY GIRL PARADE by GOLIATH BOOKS
Distributed by Freebird Publishers

PUBLISHED BY
GOLIATH

SEXY GIRL PARADE
Prison Friendly Photo Book

SEXY GIRL PARADE
Prison Friendly Photo Book

See more in SEXY GIRL PARADE by GOLIATH BOOKS
Distributed by Freebird Publishers

PUBLISHED BY
GOLIATH

Kitty Kat: Adult Entertainment Non Nude Resource Book

our gifts are made in America!

FREEBIRD PUBLISHERS
GIFTS

FREEBIRD PUBLISHERS
GIFT LOOK BOOK 2022-23
★USA

ALL IN ONE FULL COLOR BOOK!

Baby
Birthday
Care Packages
Children's Gifts
Easter
Fall Gifts
Father's Day
Gardening Gifts
Get Well
Gifts for Men
Gifts for Women
Gourmet
Halloween
Meat & Cheeses
Mini Baskets

Mother's Day
New Home
Pet Gifts
Plush
Snack Baskets
Special Diets
Specialty Foods
Sports
St. Patrick's
Sympathy
Thank You
Valentine's
Wedding & Romance
And More!

Full size, color GIFT LOOK BOOK with hundreds of our high quality handcrafted gifts to choose from, all made in the U.S.A. We offer complete line of gift baskets that have been custom designed. We have flowers that get delivered fresh in bud-form so they open up to bloom in front of your loved ones. Our chocolates are of the finest quality, all made fresh. All of our gifts are skillfully featured in detailed full color photographs.

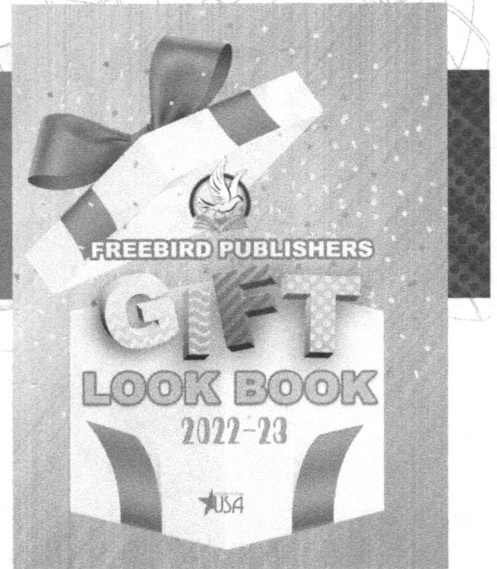

Only $19.99
FREE S/H
SOFTCOVER, 8.5" x 11", 110+ pages

with every book receive a
$19.99 voucher from our GIFT LOOK BOOK for $95.00 or more. (not including shipping & handling. good towards a purchase of any gift order

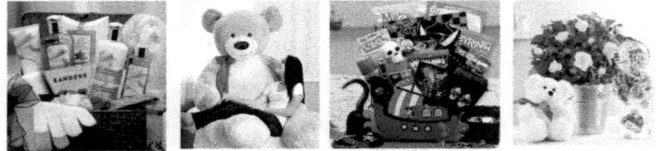

TOUCHSTONE CRYSTAL BY SWAROVSKI
SWAROVSKI CRYSTAL ON THE RED CARPET

only $9.99

Touchstone

All our jewels feature fine quality SWAROVSKI Crystals and SWAROVSKI Zirconia, the finest simulated diamond in the world.

WANT TO SEE MORE OF OUR SWAROVSKI CRYSTAL JEWELRY...

Order our full size, color catalog with hundreds of our high quality, beautifully handcrafted jewelry pieces to by Swarovski Collections that have been custom designed. Swarovski's rich heritage of craftsmanship, creativity and innovation ensures that the quality, cut and finish of every crystal is second to none. All of our jewelry is skillfully featured in detailed full color photographs on 8.5 X 11" 80 glossy pages with full descriptions & prices. Over 400 pieces of high quality jewelry and accent pieces.

How to order: on blank paper, write Touchstone Crystal Catalog, and include your complete contact info with payment of $9.99 to Freebird Publishers. All catalogs are mailed USPS tracking with packing slip/invoice.

With every catalog receive a $9.99 Voucher, good towards a purchase of Touchstone Crystal by Swarovski for $50.00 or more. (not including sales tax and S/H)

No Order Form Needed: Clearly write on paper & send with payment to:
Freebird Publishers 221 Pearl St., Ste. 541, North Dighton, MA 02764
Diane@FreebirdPublishers.com   www.Freebirdpublishers.com
We accept all forms of payment. Plus Venmo & CashApp!
Venmo: @FreebirdPublishers   CashApp: $FreebirdPublishers

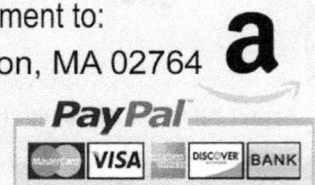

a
PayPal
MasterCard VISA AMERICAN DISCOVER BANK

By Mike Enemigo

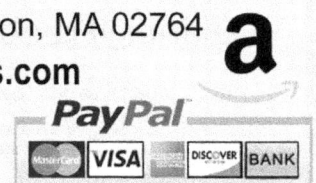

Weight Loss Unlocked

A Total Weight-Loss, Diet, and Fitness Guide

The Ultimate Guide for Losing Weight in Prison

Losing weight in the carbohydrate, sugary, processed food world of prison can seem impossible when combined with the boredom and "Groundhog Day" setup of prison. The only thing that seems to change is the food and we eat it all. Now the inmate obesity rate is higher than the 52% national average! Well now help is here! In this easy to read book, you can begin your weight loss journey TODAY!

☑ • Diet Plan

☑ • Intermittent Fasting Guides

☑ • Nutritional Facts

☑ • Packaging Information

☑ • Water Guidebook

☑ • Challenges

☑ • Real Inmate Testimonials

☑ • Full Cookbook of Healthy Meals, Deserts & Drinks that

Softcover, 6"x9", 248 Pages, B&W

WEIGHT LOSS UNLOCKED
A Total Weight-Loss, Diet, and Fitness Guide

Paul J. R. Dawson

work for all 50 states commissary!

☑ • Full Body Stretching Guide

☑ • Yoga for Beginners

☑ • Exercises for all body types you can do in cell

☑ • Motivational Quotes

☑ • And much more!

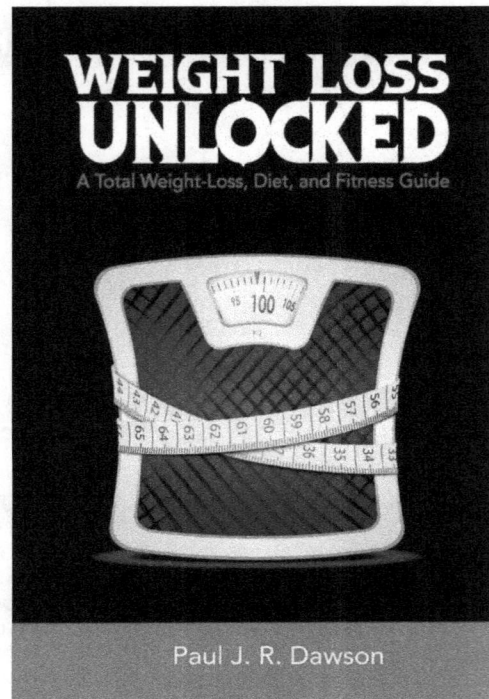

By Mike Enemigo

Kitty Kat

ADULT ENTERTAINMENT NON-NUDE RESOURCE BOOK
COMPILED BY MIKE ENEMIGO

☐ Send Me Kitty Kat - Adult Entertainment Non-Nude Resource Book $31.99

This book is jam packed with hundreds of sexy photos including photo spreads. The book contains the complete info on sexy photo sellers, hot magazines, page turning bookstore, sections on strip clubs, porn stars, alluring models, thought provoking stories and must see movies. Softcover, 8x10", Color covers, B&W interior, 185+ pages $31.99 ($24.99 plus $7 s/h)

PRICES INCLUDE SHIPPING/HANDLING WITH TRACKING

NAME: _____ Number: _____

ADDRESS: _____

CITY: _____ STATE: _____ ZIP: _____

We accept all forms of payments:

Freebird Publishers
221 Pearl St., Ste. 541
North Dighton, MA
02764
Diane@freebirdpublishers.com

Kitty Kat

ADULT ENTERTAINMENT NON-NUDE RESOURCE BOOK
COMPILED BY MIKE ENEMIGO

☐ Send Me Kitty Kat - Adult Entertainment Non-Nude Resource Book $31.99

This book is jam packed with hundreds of sexy photos including photo spreads. The book contains the complete info on sexy photo sellers, hot magazines, page turning bookstore, sections on strip clubs, porn stars, alluring models, thought provoking stories and must see movies. Softcover, 8x10", Color covers, B&W interior, 185+ pages $31.99 ($24.99 plus $7 s/h)

PRICES INCLUDE SHIPPING/HANDLING WITH TRACKING

NAME: _____ Number: _____

ADDRESS: _____

CITY: _____ STATE: _____ ZIP: _____

We accept all forms of payments:

Freebird Publishers
221 Pearl St., Ste. 541
North Dighton, MA
02764
Diane@freebirdpublishers.com

Kitty Kat

ADULT ENTERTAINMENT NON-NUDE RESOURCE BOOK
COMPILED BY MIKE ENEMIGO

☐ Send Me Kitty Kat - Adult Entertainment Non-Nude Resource Book $31.99

This book is jam packed with hundreds of sexy photos including photo spreads. The book contains the complete info on sexy photo sellers, hot magazines, page turning bookstore, sections on strip clubs, porn stars, alluring models, thought provoking stories and must see movies. Softcover, 8x10", Color covers, B&W interior, 185+ pages $31.99 ($24.99 plus $7 s/h)

PRICES INCLUDE SHIPPING/HANDLING WITH TRACKING

NAME: _____ Number: _____

ADDRESS: _____

CITY: _____ STATE: _____ ZIP: _____

We accept all forms of payments:

Freebird Publishers
221 Pearl St., Ste. 541
North Dighton, MA
02764
Diane@freebirdpublishers.com

Kitty Kat: Adult Entertainment Non Nude Resource Book

FREEBIRD PUBLISHERS
PEN PAL BOOKS

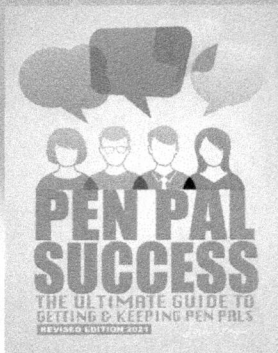

Only $31.99
Includes S/H with Tracking
SOFTCOVER, 8" x 10", 260 pages

You've heard it said "The game is to be sold not told." Well, now a new book is doing all the telling about the game.
In 20 information-dense chapters you'll DISCOVER the following secrets:

• How to find FREE pen pals that are willing to write to prisoners.
• Make money legally in the pen pal game without running any bogus prison scams!
• Effectively use online pen pal websites.
• What to do once you get your pen pal so you can them on your team for years!
• How to write letters to pen pals that get you responses!
• Learn the website the author used to get 20+ hits in the first week his profile was up.
• How to rekindle a lost pen pal correspondence and keep pen pals coming back for more.
• The act of gift giving so you don't look like a trick-off artist;

What's more, this book is jam-packed with the full contact information of people and companies that can help you succeed today!

AND THERE'S MUCH, MUCH MORE!

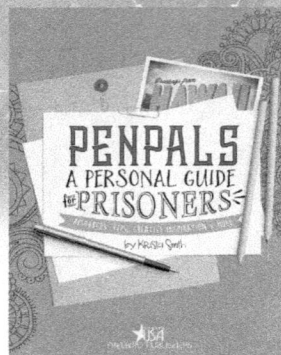

Only $31.99
Includes S/H with Tracking
SOFTCOVER, 8" x 10", 200 pages

Resources, Tips, Creative Inspiration and much more!
A guide designed to help prisoners keep their pen pals interested and coming back for more. With resources, tips, and creative inspiration you're sure to hang on to your pen pals.

• Pen Pal Resources for Prisoners
• Pen Pal Resources for Anyone
• Pen Pal Specialized Resources
• Pen Pal Profiles & Writing Tips
• Creating Your Profile
• Writing Your First Letter
• Pen Pal Etiquette
• 100 Things to Tell Your Pen Pal
• 100 Getting to Know You Questions
• How to Keep It Interesting
• How to Improve Your Handwriting
• How to Start & Close Your Letter
• How to Write a Love Letter
• Pen Pal Mail Art & Ideas
• Envelope Art & Ideas
• Fonts / Lettering
• Hand Lettering
• Doodles & Embellishments
• Make Your Own Greeting Cards
• The Art of Origami
• Quotes to Share with Your Pen Pal
• Pen Pal Stationary
• My Pen Pal Notes & Address Book Section

No Order Form Needed: Clearly write on paper & send with payment to:

Freebird Publishers 221 Pearl St., Ste 541, North Dighton, MA 02764

Diane@FreebirdPublishers.com   www.Freebirdpublishers.com

We accept all forms of payment. Plus Venmo & CashApp!
Venmo: @FreebirdPublishers   CashApp: $FreebirdPublishers

a

PayPal
MasterCard VISA DISCOVER BANK

By Mike Enemigo

PENACON

Penacon is owned and operated by Freebird Publishers, your trusted inmate service provider.

Penacon.com dedicated to assisting the imprisoned community find connections of friendship and romance around the world. Your profile will be listed on our user-friendly website. We make sure your profile is seen at the highest visibility rate available by driving traffic to our site by consistent advertising and networking. We know how important it is to have your ad seen by as many people as possible in order to bring you the best service possible. Pen pals can now email their first message through penacon.com! We print and send these messages with return addresses if you get one. We value your business and process profiles promptly.

To receive your informational package and application send two stamps to:

PENACON

221 Pearl St., Ste. 533
North Dighton, MA 02764
Penacon@freebirdpublishers.com
Corrlinks: diane@freebirdpublishers.com
JPay: diane@freebirdpublishers.com

By Mike Enemigo

FULL COLOR CATALOG 92-PAGES FILLED WITH BOOKS, GIFTS AND SERVICES.

CATALOG ONLY $5 - SHIPS BY FIRST CLASS MAIL

Kitty Kat: Adult Entertainment Non Nude Resource Book

FREEBIRD PUBLISHERS

Pro Se Collection by Raymond E. Lumsden

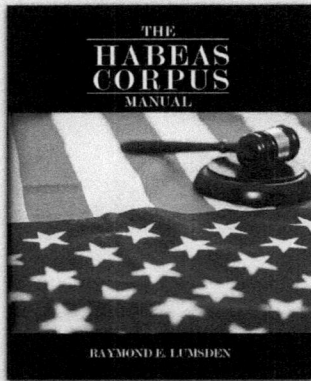

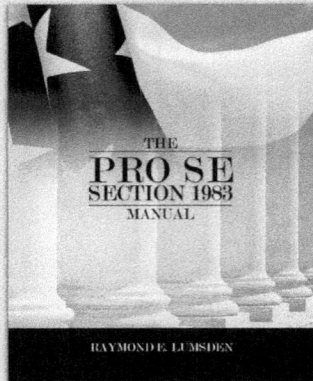

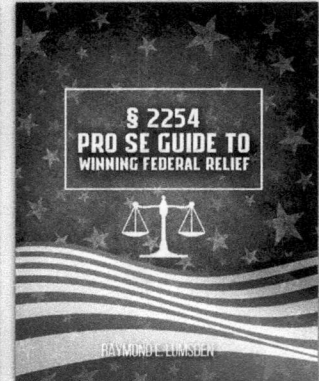

This legal collection is the no-nonsense, easy to understand, and effective work by one of Freebird Publisher's Best Selling Legal Authors, Raymond E. Lumsden. Specifically written by an inmate with extensive legal training and education, for inmates seeking relief in the twisting and confusing legal system of America.

★ Easy to follow instructions;
★ Dozens of sample motions and pleadings;
★ Up to date case citings and writings;
★ **5** Star Amazon Ratings;
★ Numerous success stories of relief being obtained, etc.

A MUST HAVE COLLECTION FOR ANY PRO SE USER!!!

We accept all forms of payment!

★ COMING SOON ★
- *The Pro Se Guide to Parole*
- *"DNA": Proving Your Innocence*

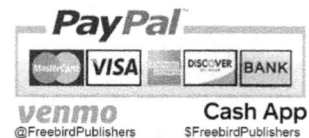

PayPal
MasterCard | VISA | DISCOVER | BANK
venmo @FreebirdPublishers | Cash App $FreebirdPublishers

By Mike Enemigo

FREEBIRD PUBLISHERS

The Millionaire Prisoner's Collection

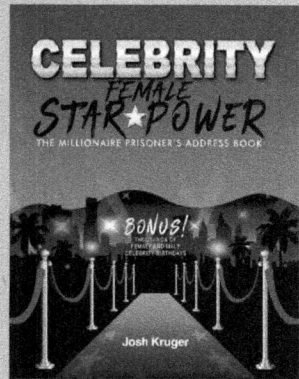

The Millionaire Prisoner and Freebird Publishers bring you Josh Kruger's latest books from earning money from your cell to connecting with pen pals and celebrities.

Cellpreneur: The Millionaire Prisoner's Guidebook $31.99
This book is only for those prisoners who want to achieve their business dreams! ... Every word is designed so that prisoners can succeed now!

Prison Picasso: The Millionaire Prisoner's Way to Sell Arts/Crafts $35.99
Wish you could sell art patterns to greeting card companies for $400? Want to know the magazine that pays over $4,000 for artwork they like? Are you tired of trading your art/crafts for just typical commissary scraps? Want to know where to go online to find 130,000+ people who like prison arts and crafts? Then this book was written for you!

Pen Pal Success: The Ultimate Guide to Getting and Keeping Pen Pals $31.99
You have never seen a pen pal resource this detail on what it takes to succeed in the pen pal game today! Written by lifer, Josh Kruger author of The Millionaire Prisoner. Pen Pal Success contains "insider's" wisdom especially for prisoners.

Celebrity Female Star Power: The Millionaire Prisoner's Address Book $36.99
Want to contact your favorite female celebrity? Ever wished you could write for a free photo, get an autograph, or letter back? But you didn't know how or where to send your letter? Well, now you can because this book shows you how!

Prices above Include Shipping & Handling.

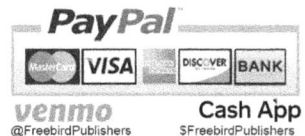

We accept all forms of payment!

PayPal — MasterCard VISA DISCOVER BANK
venmo @FreebirdPublishers
Cash App $FreebirdPublishers

For more info on each book, order our catalog!

CATALOG ONLY $5 - SHIPS BY FIRST CLASS MAIL
We have created four different versions of our new catalog A: Complete B:No Pen Pal Content C:No Sexy Photo Content D:No Pen Pal and Sexy Content. Available in full Color or B&W (please specify) please make sure you order the correct catalog based on your prison mail room regulations. We are not responsible for rejected or lost in the mail catalogs. Send SASE for payment by stamp options.
ADDITIONAL OPTION: add $5 for Shipping with Tracking

NO ORDER FORM NEEDED CLEARLY WRITE ON PAPER & SEND PAYMENT TO:
FREEBIRD PUBLSIHERS 221 Pearl St., Ste. 541, North Dighton, MA 02764
www.Freebird Publishers.com Diane@FreebirdPublishers.com Text/Phone: 774-406-8682

Kitty Kat: Adult Entertainment Non Nude Resource Book

Thanks for your interest in
Freebird Publishers!

We value our customers and would love to hear from you! Reviews are an important part in bringing you quality publications. We love hearing from our readers-rather it's good or bad (though we strive for the best)!

If you could take the time to review/rate any publication you've purchased with Freebird Publishers we would appreciate it!

If your loved one uses Amazon, have them post your review on the books you've read. This will help us tremendously, in providing future publications that are even more useful to our readers and growing our business.

Amazon works off of a 5 star rating system. When having your loved one rate us be sure to give them your chosen star number as well as a written review. Though written reviews aren't required, we truly appreciate hearing from you.

☆ ☆ ☆ ☆ ☆ **Everything a prisoner needs is available in this book.**
January 30, 201 June 7, 2018
Format: Paperback

A necessary reference book for anyone in prison today. This book has everything an inmate needs to keep in touch with the outside world on their own from inside their prison cell. Inmate Shopper's business directory provides complete contact information on hundreds of resources for inmate services and rates the companies listed too! The book has even more to offer, contains numerous sections that have everything from educational, criminal justice, reentry, LGBT, entertainment, sports schedules and more. The best thing is each issue has all new content and updates to keep the inmate informed on todays changes. We recommend everybody that knows anyone in prison to send them a copy, they will thank you.

By Mike Enemigo

FREEBIRD PUBLISHERS
REFERENCE BOOKS

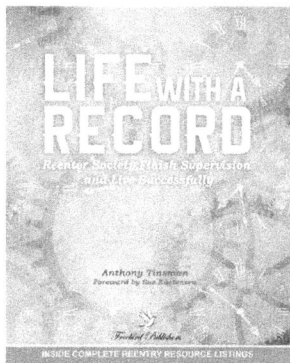

Only $34.99
includes S/H with Tracking
SOFTCOVER, 8" x 10", 360 pages

Things don't magically change after you get kicked out of prison. Life starts all over again but there's a catch, having a record impacts almost every part of your life. With this book you'll find out how to prepare for life as an ex-offender. Filled with insights, advice, contacts, and exercises the information strikes legal, personal and professional levels. A real world guide for minimizing disruptions and maximizing success. Life With A Record helps make sense of the major challenges facing ex-offenders today. Ten hard hitting chapters outline the purpose of making a Strategic Reentry Plan and making peace with supervisors, family, your community and your future.
Inside you will find: How to rebuild your credit, halfway house rules and terms, special grants and loans to finance education, job training or start a business, legal tips for dealing with discrimination, hundreds of reentry contacts and so much more!

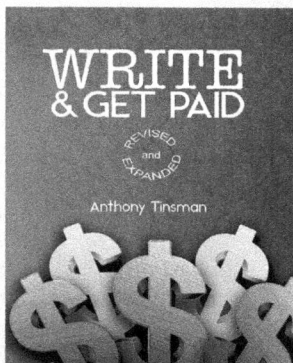

Only $31.99
includes S/H with Tracking
SOFTCOVER, 8" x 10", 240+ pages

Don't let a prison cell keep you from interacting with the world. Jailhouse publishing is possible! In fact, our new book gives authors the blueprint for first time to full time success.
In 30 information-dense chapters you'll DISCOVER how to turn your way with words into wads of cash.
• How to brainstorm, outline and then write your book.
• What to negotiate for in publishing agreements and other binding documents!
• Learn to write one book but sell it in multiple formats.
• Effectively make yourself irresisstable to editors–who'll stay on your team for years.
• What to do once you get published so your readers keep coming back.
• Learn self-publishing tools on Amazon, iTunes, Scrivener and beyond.
• Find useful creative writing advice
• How to design a press kit that empowers your publicity campaign
• And more!

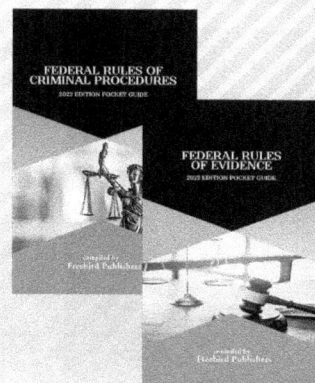

Only $30.99 for both
includes S/H with Tracking
SOFTCOVER, 8" x 10", 210+ pages

First adopted in 1975, the Federal Rules of Evidence codify the evidence law that applies in United States federal courts. In addition, many states in the United States have either adopted the Federal Rules of Evidence, with or without local variations, or have revised their own evidence rules or codes to at least partially follow the federal rules.
In general, the purpose of rules of evidence is to regulate the evidence that the jury may use to reach a verdict.
The Federal Rules of Criminal Procedure govern how federal criminal prosecutions are conducted in United States district courts and the general trial courts of the U.S. government. The admissibility and use of evidence in crimi- nal proceedings (as well as civil) is governed by the separate Federal Rules of Evidence.
The rules are promulgated by the Supreme Court of the United States, pursuant to its statu- tory authority.

No Order Form Needed: Clearly write on paper & send with payment to:

Freebird Publishers 221 Pearl St., Ste. 541, North Dighton, MA 02764

Diane@FreebirdPublishers.com   www.Freebirdpublishers.com

We accept all forms of payment. Plus Venmo & CashApp!
Venmo: @FreebirdPublishers   CashApp: $FreebirdPublishers

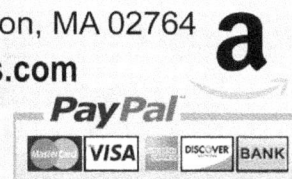

PayPal
MasterCard VISA DISCOVER BANK

FREEBIRD PUBLISHERS
REFERENCE BOOKS

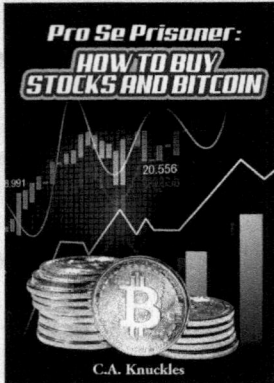

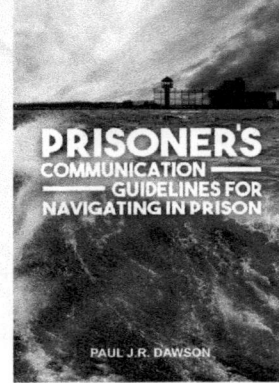

Only $26.99	Only $26.99	Only $23.99
includes S/H with tracking **SOFTCOVER, 6" x 9", 175+ pages**	**includes S/H with tracking** **SOFTCOVER, 8" x 10", 240+ pages**	**includes S/H with tracking** **SOFTCOVER, 6" x 9", 200+ pages**

Being a Pro Se Prisoner is a mindset. Do it yourself prisoners who go and get knowledge, money and freedom. We were told that prison and DOC would rehabilitate us with programs, school, and re-entry programs. That hasn't happened, and as such the system hasn't served its purpose. With this book you will have taken the first step to empowering yourself to become financially free. Pro Se Prisoner: How to Buy Stocks & Bitcoin will allow you to learn about your financial freedom, investment options, how to buy DRIPS's, cryptocurrency and ETF's. These pages are more than a book they're the start of your journey into different investments that you probably thought weren't available to you until now. In prison you can buy stocks, bitcoins, and ETF's without having people on the outside lying to you about not having the time to help. Become a Pro Se Prisoner and put the power back into your hands.

Success in life is about becoming what you want to be. You may have heard money is the root of all evil, I don't believe that this is the case. Some people do not truly understand the concept of money. As an adult, I now realize that there is nothing wrong with wanting to be financially free, rich, or wealthy. If you also desire this then it only means that you crave a wealthier, fuller, and more abundant life than what you are currently enduring.

To become financially successful, you need to stop thinking of spending and think more on investing and acquiring assets. If not then you will continue to stay in the typical lifestyle of working for money, paying taxes, and hoping that circumstances will change (i.e., hitting the lottery or getting a substantial raise in pay). Once you begin to see money for what it is, a tool to invest, you can begin to achieve greater financial success.
Covering: Credit, Investing, Trading, Real Estate, Asset Protection and more!

Being incarcerated is hard enough on its own without dealing with the other inmates, this is where most of the stress comes from while incarcerated. HELP IS HERE! In this new book, Prisoner's Communication Guideline for Navigating in Prison has years of experience, knowledge and research on every page.Prisoners from all over the country have contributed unique points of view and successful strategies for verbally and non-verbally existing in prison during your sentence and return to society.

Whether you are truly interested in becoming an effective communicator or just improving your skills, this is the book for you. Apply the topics discussed in this book and be able to earn more privileges, make more money and get along better with fellow convicts and staff alike. Do not delay any longer, get started today. Really apply yourself and you are bound for success!

By Mike Enemigo

Freebird Publishers
Post-Conviction Relief Series

Post-Conviction Relief Books

⇒ Secrets Exposed

⇒ The Appeal

⇒ Advancing Your Claim

⇒ Winning Claims

⇒ C.O.A. in the Supreme Court

⇒ Post-Conviction Relief Second Last Chance

JUST ARRIVED

Post-Conviction Relief: The Advocate

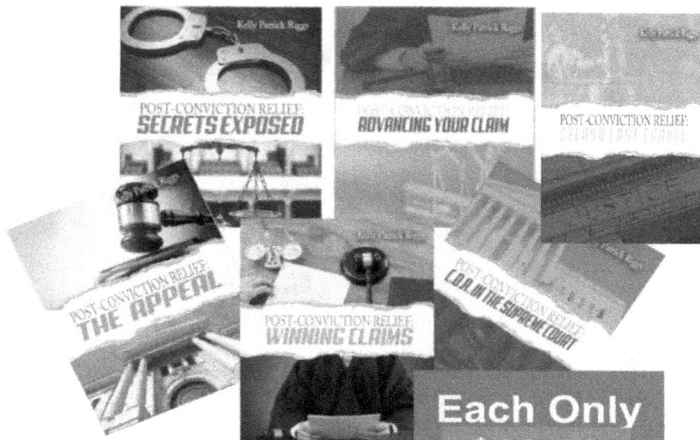

Each Only $28.99 Includes S/H with tracking

Post-Conviction Relief is a subject most often pursued only by prisoners, the people who are most deprived of the necessary information. What is offered in most law libraries, is in inadequate, because what is needed is watered down by piles of useless and confusing information. That's why the Post-Conviction Relief series was written. It is a no-nonsense guide, to legal research, that is written in a language that anyone can understand. Most importantly, each book has been written to serve a specific purpose, as instructions for a specific step in the Post-Conviction process. With this collection of books, the average person can quickly become a more powerful advocate than they have ever been before, even if only on their own case. Within this set of books, the reader will find that there is something for all prisoners, whether it's their first day in prison or their first day of supervised release.

★ The best instruction one can receive is the words of experience. The Post-Conviction Relief series is written by a real advocate who has actually been there and prevailed in many cases.

★ In most cases prisoners have only one year to make their claims, the Post-Conviction Relief series is the no-nonsense path to understanding the process.

★ The Post-Conviction Relief series provides its readers with the court rules that pertain to Post Conviction Relief. A great resource for prisoners who are often locked down.

★ Post-Conviction Relief: you want to succeed, follow my lead.

★ All books are not created equal. Get only what you need with the Post-Conviction Relief series.

All Books Softcover, 8x10", B&W, 190+ pages EACH $28.99 includes s/h with tracking

Written in simple terms for everyone to understand, it's not just for lawyers anymore.

NO ORDER FORM NEEDED CLEARLY WRITE ON PAPER & SEND PAYMENT TO:

Freebird Publishers 221 Pearl St., Ste. 541, North Dighton, MA 02764

Diane@FreebirdPublishers.com   www.FreebirdPublishers.com
Toll Free: 888-712-1987   Text/Phone: 774-406-8682

amazon.com

PayPal   VISA   DISCOVER   BANK

We Accept All Forms of Payment PLUS Venmo & Cash App
Venmo Address @FreebirdPublishers Cash App Address #FreebirdPublishers

Kitty Kat: Adult Entertainment Non Nude Resource Book

FREEBIRD PUBLISHERS
Cook Books

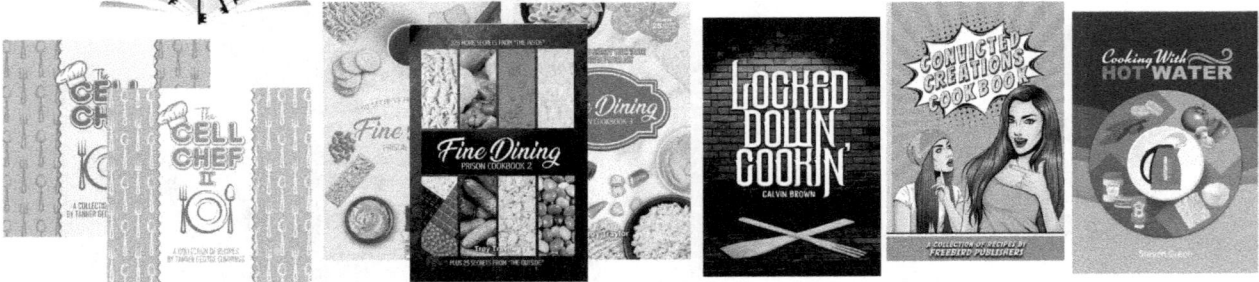

Cell Chef I: Eating the same thing day in and out? Tired of the same boring, bland tasting food? Cell Chef is filled with hundreds of fantastic recipes, simply made with everyday common comissary/store foods. - Meals, Snacks, Sauces, Spreads, Dips, Drinks, Sweet Desserts **$20.99**
Cell Chef II: Completely different and yummier than the past - all new recipes in the Cell Chef's second book. Includes Meals, spreads, sandwiches, sauces, dips, drinks and sweets. **$20.99**
Cell Chef Bundle: Get Cell Chef I and Cell Chef II for the great deal of **$36.99**

Fine Dining 1: Developed by prisoners for prisoners. Cook a delicous, tasty meal with ordinary low-cost ingredients. Tasty drinks, condiments, dips, side dishes, snacks, gumbos, chowders, meals, pizzas, mexican delights, cakes and pies, cheesecakes, and sweets of all kinds. **$22.99**
Fine Dining 2: Ready to be the talk of your unit and discover your creative side at the same time. Over 250 exciting and fun ways to create whatever you're craving in Fine Dining's second book. Including Drinks, dips, soups, beef, chicken, fish, mexican, pizzas, breakfast, pies, cakes, treats, fudge, cookies, pudding and so much more. Bonus content included. **$27.99**
Fine Dining 3: The 3rd and final book in the Fine Dining Prison Cookbook series. Eating healthy in prison can be a challenge. Prison foods are full of starch and many other things. However many comissaries are now beginning to offer healthier choices. The Fine Dining Prison Cookbook 3 has all you need to prepare the healthiest options available to you. Only **$27.99**
Fine Dining Bundle: Fine Dining 1 and 2. Two great books at a great cost. Only **$41.98**

Locked Down Cookin': A culinary touch on prison commissary and prison meal trays. Culinary touch, "The Big Cal Way." **$22.99**

Convicted Creations Cook Book: Just because you're behind bars, doesn't mean your cravings for home-cooked foods are any less real. With these recipes you'll be able to enjoy the flavors of a good meal. Includes: Drinks, Dips, Sauces, Main Dishes, Sweets and Treats! **$21.99**

Cooking With Hot Water: Tired of prison cookbooks that require a microwave, stinger, hotplate, or any other cooking device? The only thing needed for the recipes in this book is hot (190°) water. Recipe categories include: Drinks, sauces, dips, rice dishes, ramon dishes, bagels, snacks, pizza, mexican food, asian dishes, desserts, frostings, and so much more! **$27.99**

By Mike Enemigo

Kitty Kat: Adult Entertainment Non Nude Resource Book

THE BEST RESOURCE DIRECTORY FOR PRISONERS, $19.99 & $7.00 S/H: This book has over 1,450 resources for prisoners! Includes: Pen-Pal Com- panies! Non-Nude Photo Sellers! Free Books and Other Publications! Legal Assistance! Prisoner Advocates! Prisoner Assistants! Correspondence Education! Money-Making Opportunities! Resources for Prison Writers, Poets, Artists, and much, much more! Anything you can think of doing from your prison cell, this book contains the re- sources to do it!

THE PRISON MANUAL: $19.99 & $7.00 S/H : The Prison Manual is your all-in-one book on how to not only survive the rough terrain of the American prison system, but use it to your advantage so you can THRIVE from it! How to Use Your Prison Time to YOUR Advantage; How to Write Letters that Will Give You Maximum Effec- tiveness; Workout and Physical Health Secrets that Will Keep You as FIT as Possible; The Psychological impact of incarceration and How to Maintain Your MAXIMUM Level of Mental Health; Prison Art Techniques; Fulfilling Food Recipes; Parole Preparation Strategies and much, MUCH more!

THE ART & POWER OF LETTER WRITING FOR PRISONERS DELUXE EDITION, $16.95 & $5.00 S/H: When locked inside a prison cell, being able to write well is one of the most powerful skills you can have. Some of the most famous and powerful men in the world are known for letters they've written from inside their prison cells, such as: Martin Luther King; Malcolm X; Nelson Mandella; George Jackson; and perhaps the most famous and powerful of all, Apostle Paul, who's letters are in the Bible!

PRETTY GIRLS LOVE BAD BOYS: THE PRISONER'S GUIDE TO GETTING GIRLS, $16.95 & $5.00 S/H: Tired of the same, boring, cliché pen pal books that don't tell you what you really need to know? If so, this book is for you! Anything you need to know on the art of long and short distance seduction is included within these pages! Not only does it give you the science of attracting pen pals from websites, it also includes psychological profiles and instructions on how to seduce any woman you set your sights on! Includes interviews of women who have fallen in love with prisoners, bios for pen pal ads, pre-written love letters, romantic poems, love-song lyrics, jokes and much, much more! This book is the ultimate guide - a must-have for any prisoner who refuses to let prison walls affect their MAC'n.

THE LADIES WHO LOVE PRISONERS, $12.00 & $4.00 S/H: New Special Report reveals the secrets of real women who have fallen in love with prisoners, regardless of crime, sentence, or location. This info will give you a HUGE advantage in getting girls from prison.

RAW LAW, $15.00 & $5.00 S/H: TIRED OF FEELING POWERLESS BECAUSE UNSCRUPULOUS GUARDS HAVE VIOLATED YOUR RIGHTS WITHOUT FEAR OF CONSEQUENCE? THEN THIS BOOK IS FOR YOU! Raw Law For Prisoners is a clear and concise guide for prisoners and their advocates to understanding civil rights laws guaranteed to prisoners under the US Constitution, and how to successfully file a lawsuit when those rights have been violated! From initial complaint to trial, this book will take you through the entire process, step by step, in simple, easy-to-understand terms. Also included are several examples where prisoners have sued prison officials successfully, resulting in changes of unjust rules and regulations and recourse for rights violations, oftentimes resulting in rewards of thousands, even mil- lions of dollars in damages! If you feel your rights have been violated, don't lash out at guards, which is usually ineffective and only makes matters worse. Instead, defend yourself successfully by using the legal system, and getting the power of the courts on your side!

GET OUT, STAY OUT!, $16.95 & $5.00 S/H: This book should be in the hands of everyone in a prison cell. It reveals a challenging but clear course for overcoming the obstacles that stand between prisoners and their freedom. For those behind bars, one goal outshines all others: GETTING OUT! After being released, that goal then shifts to STAYING OUT! This book will help prisoners do both. It has been masterfully constructed into five parts that will help prisoners maximize focus while they strive to accomplish whichever goal is at hand.

THE CEO MANUAL: HOW TO START A BUSINESS WHEN YOU GET OUT OF PRISON, $16.95 & $5.00 S/H: This new book will teach you the simplest way to start your own business when you get out of prison. Includes: Start-up Steps! The Secrets to Pulling Money from Investors! How to Manage People Effectively! How To Legally Protect Your Assets from "them"! Hundreds of resources to get you started, including a list of 'loan friendly" banks! (ALSO PUBLISHED AS CEO MANUAL: START A BUSINESS, BE A BOSS!)

GET OUT, GET RICH: HOW TO GET PAID LEGALLY WHEN YOU GET OUT OF PRISON, $16.95 & $5.00 S/H: Many of you are incarcerated for a money-moti- vated crime. But w/ today's tech & opportunities, not only is the crime-for-money risk/reward ratio not strategically wise, it's not even necessary. You can earn much more money by partaking in anyone of the easy, legal hustles explained in this book, regardless of your record. Help yourself earn an honest income so you can not only make a lot of money, but say good-bye to penitentiary chances and prison forever! (Note: Many things in this book can even he done from inside prison.) (ALSO PUB- LISHED AS HOOD MILLIONAIRE: HOW TO HUSTLE AND WIN LEGALLY!)

THE MONEY MANUAL: UNDERGROUND CASH SECRETS EXPOSED! $16.95 & $5.00 S/H: Becoming a millionaire is equal parts what you make, and what you don't spend -- AKA save. All Millionaires and Billionaires have mastered the art of not only making money, but keeping the money they make (remember Donald Trump's tax maneuvers?), as well as establishing credit so that they are loaned money by banks and trusted with money from investors: AKA OPM -- other people's money. And did you know there are millionaires and billionaires just waiting to GIVE money away? It's true! These are all very-little known secrets 'they" don't want YOU to know about, but that I'm exposing in my new book!

THE MILLIONAIRE PRISONER SPECIAL 2-in-1 EDITION, $24.99 & $7.00 S/H: Why wait until you get out of prison to achieve your dreams? Here's a blueprint that you can use to become successful! The Millionaire Prisoner is your complete reference to overcoming any obstacle in prison. You won't be able to put it down! With this book you will discover the secrets to: Making money from your cell! Become an expert on any topic! Develop the habits of the rich! Network with celebrities! Set up your own website! Market your products, ideas and services and much, much more!

THE MILLIONAIRE 3: SUCCESS UNIVERSITY, $16.95 & $5.00 S/H: Why wait until you get out of prison to achieve your dreams? Here's a new-look blueprint that you can use to be successful! The Millionaire Prisoner 3 contains advanced strategies to overcoming any obstacle in prison. You won't be able to put it down! The TMP program has enabled thousands of prisoners to succeed and it will show you the way also!

THE MILLIONAIRE 4: PEN PAL MASTERY, $16.95 & $5.00 S/H: Tired of subpar results? Here's a master blueprint that you can use to get tons of pen pals! *TMP 4: Pen Pal Mastery* is your complete roadmap to finding your one true love. You won't be able to put it down! With this book you'll DISCOVER the SECRETS to: Get FREE pen pals & which sites are best to use; Successful tactics female prisoners can win with;   Use astrology to find love; friendship & more; Build a winning social media presence; Playing phone tag & successful sex talk; Hidden benefits of foreign pen pals; Find your success mentors; Turning "hits" into friendships; Learn how to write let- ters/emails that get results. All of this and much more!

THE MILLIONAIRE PRISONER 5: FREE MONEY: $24.99 & $7 S/H: Seeking an end to your money problems? Look no further! Here's a master blueprint that reveals all that's available! *TMP 5: FREE MONEY* is your complete roadmap to finding all the FREE Money options out there for convicts. You won't be able to put it down! With this book you'll DISCOVER the SECRETS to:1. Getting FREE Money for incarcerated veterans; 2. What grants are available for artists & writers; 3. FREE Money for col- lege classes that you NEVER have to pay back; 4. Use crowdfunding to get Money for your business projects; 5. How to travel the world & get paid for doing it; 6. Find FREE public information that you can use & sell; 7. Build your personal credit and get FREE Money bonuses; 8. Where to get FREE legal assistance from; 9. Help your baby mama get FREE stuff for her & the kids; 10. One website that will show you what's available just for you. All of this and much more! This book shows you where and how.

JAILHOUSE PUBLISHING: $19.99 & $7.00 S/H: In 2010, after flirting with the idea for two years, Mike Enemigo started writing his first book. In 2014, he officially launched his publishing company, The Cell Block, with the release of five books. Of course, with no mentor(s), how-to guides, or any real resources, he was met with fail- ure after failure as he tried to navigate the treacherous goal of publishing books from his prison cell. However, he was determined to make it. He was determined to figure it out and he refused to quit. In Mike's new book, Jailhouse Publishing for Money, Power, and Fame, he breaks down all his jailhouse publishing secrets and strategies, so you can do all he's done, but without the trials and tribulations he's had to go through...

To order, send money order or institutional check to:

THE CELL BLOCK • PO BOX 1025 • RANCHO CORDOVA , CA 95741
For more info, visit thecellblock.net now!

By Mike Enemigo

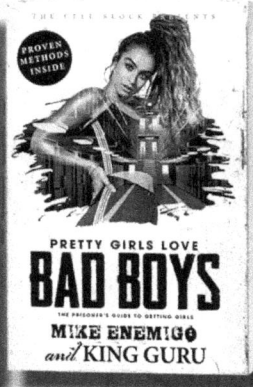

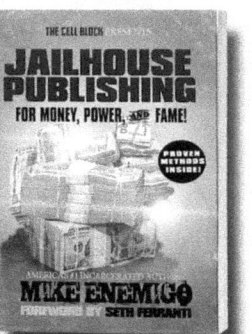

2 MUST HAVE
BOOKS FOR PRISONERS

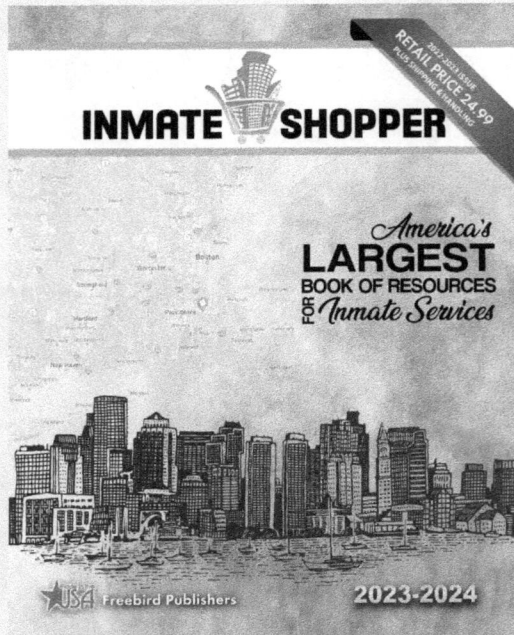

INMATE SHOPPER

RETAIL PRICE 24.99
PLUS SHIPPING & HANDLING

America's
LARGEST
BOOK OF RESOURCES
FOR Inmate Services

USA Freebird Publishers

2023-2024

$29.99
$20.99 plus $9 Shipping/Handling
with Tracking

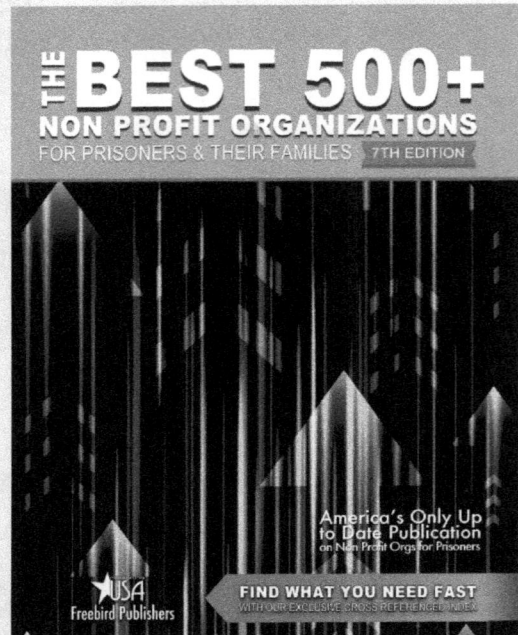

THE BEST 500+
NON PROFIT ORGANIZATIONS
FOR PRISONERS & THEIR FAMILIES 7TH EDITION

America's Only Up
to Date Publication
on Non Profit Orgs for Prisoners

FIND WHAT YOU NEED FAST
WITH OUR EXCLUSIVE CROSS REFERENCED INDEX

USA
Freebird Publishers

$26.99
$17.99 plus $9 Shipping/Handling
with Tracking

NO ORDER FORM NEEDED
Clearly write on paper and send with payment.
Freebird Publishers, 221 Pearl St., Ste. 541, North Dighton, MA 02764

INMATE SHOPPER

EVERY ISSUE CONTAINS

Non-Nude Girls
Pen Pal Resources
Social Media
Magazine Sellers
Text/Phone
Catalogs to Order
Sexy Photo Sellers
Typists
Personal Assistants
Gift Shops
Publishing Services
LGBTQ Resources

GET BOTH
FOR JUST **$47.99** INCLUDES PRIORITY
S/H WITH TRACKING

ORDER THE COMBO & SAVE!!
$$

THE BEST 500+

Legal: Innocence, Research,
Advocates, Copies
Newsletters
Educational
Health & Healthcare
Reentry & Jobs
Family & Children
Veterans
Sentencing Issues
LGBTQ Resources
Newsletter & Books
& Much Much More!

INCLUDES MANY **RESOURCES**

ALSO AVAILABLE FOR PURCHASE AT FREEBIRDPUBLISHERS.COM

Kitty Kat: Adult Entertainment Non Nude Resource Book

www.ingramcontent.com/pod-product-compliance
Lightning Source LLC
Chambersburg PA
CBHW080241270326
41926CB00020B/4323